A MILLENNIAL
IN PARADISE

WILL CONQUER

Carlo Acutis

A MILLENNIAL
IN PARADISE

TRANSLATED BY
JAMES HENRI MCMURTRIE

SOPHIA INSTITUTE PRESS
MANCHESTER, NEW HAMPSHIRE

Cover and pictograms: Caroline Soulères.

Photos courtesy of the Acutis family; four landscapes courtesy of Wikimedia Commons.

Composition: Soft Office

paperback ISBN 978-1-64413-484-9

ebook ISBN 978-1-64413-485-6

Library of Congress Control Number: 2021934487

Second printing

To France.
To Juliana.
To Jacques and Gabriella.

"For to such belongs the kingdom of heaven."
(Matt. 19:14)

Contents

Acknowledgments

To Carlo, who helps me to continue to believe in the holiness of adolescence;

To my parents, godfather, and godmother, and the priests who accompanied me in these decisive years of my life;

To my friends, and to our ongoing exchanges, sharing, and adventures, which remind us how much we have to love life;

To Louis-Antoine, Pierre, and Benoît;

To Grégory and Pierre, who initiated this project. To Aurore and Clotilde who were able to complete it and whose encouragement and corrections allowed this book to turn out well;

To Antonia Salzano Acutis for her testimony of friendship and faith;

To Nicola Gori for his in-depth work and kindness;

To Jesus through Mary.

Fr. Will Conquer

A big, warm thank you to Fr. Will Conquer. He accepted the challenge, which was instigated on a café terrace on the other side of the world, to write the very inspiring spiritual biography of a young man for today's youth.

Thank you for your attentiveness and zeal in this work and for being so available in this year prior to your departure on a mission.

Be assured that our prayers will accompany you in Cambodia.

Many thanks also to the Acutis family for Carlo's precious memories. His yearning to be holy has carried us through all of this work's editing. May this yearning be very attractive to France's youth. We sincerely hope so.

Les Éditions Première Partie

Instructions

Dear reader, throughout these pages, you will find pictograms that will guide your reading. Allow Carlo Acutis' life to resonate in you. Become a twenty-first-century saint.

This pictogram marks the historical events that took place during Carlo's life. They will resonate with you if you have also experienced them. If you were not there during the "Y2K bug," i.e., the computer concerns related to Y2K, it's no big deal. You will quickly understand that Carlo chose to be uncompromisingly holy in a world that is not so different from ours.

You have guessed it. These are the biographical elements of Carlo's life. Before being a millennial and a geek, Carlo was, first of all, a child, and then an adolescent who shared many challenges with you. He has a true secret to show you — the keys to ordinary holiness. Like him, take up this daily challenge as well.

Carlo was a witness of God's love from his early childhood up until his last breath. This pictogram will introduce you to the key people that nourished Carlo's faith and the faces of the people who were touched and transformed by his friendship with Jesus, and his school friends — including the nurse — who were at his side during his passage to Heaven. Allow this attractive love of Christ to reach you.

By declaring Carlo Acutis to be Venerable in 2018, Pope Francis proclaimed to the world how heroically this young adolescent practiced Christian virtues — nothing less! Strength, hope, temperance, charity, prudence, justice, and faith are part of a great program. Throughout the chapters, learn these seven virtues better and put them into action in your own life, so that you too can become a hero of the faith through the Holy Spirit.

Rediscover some questions here that are personally addressed to you. This tool kit is a sort of a tailor-made examination of conscience that will allow you to embrace this plan of love that God has for you personally. Let there be no more hang-ups. Ordinary holiness is within the reach of every one of us!

Here, a biblical passage will be offered to you to nourish your reflection. Do you know that Carlo first started reading with his children's Bible? Get into the habit of reading the Word of God as well and discover how much it dwells in and supports each event in your life.

Finally, you will find a prayer that is connected to each virtue. This text is a support that is offered to help you grow in your relationship with God. But you can also invent your own prayer. Take advantage of it. The connection to Paradise in ultra-speed is free, and it is not just for this month! Carlo really understood this. The Wi-Fi password is "the Holy Spirit." Connect to Him in Heaven.

Preface

Speaking to young people today about Carlo Acutis is easy, but rather risky for the one who speaks on his behalf. It is nearly impossible to testify about his life without being challenged in our own lives. I have experienced this! When we start talking about Carlo, his example becomes more and more present. His image keeps coming back to mind like a *boomerang*. Carlo is a sign of contradiction for today's societies, which are only acquainted with the values that the media serve them every day.

It is certainly unusual to talk about virtues, as Fr. Will Conquer does. He is a young priest who was a missionary in Southeast Asia recently. To remind ourselves that there are virtues in a world of superficiality and ephemera is undoubtedly a courageous act that deserves to be admired. This choice comes from the burning heart of a missionary who wants to announce the gospel to those who are far from Christ, the Faith, and the Church. The new generations are among those who are the furthest away from them. In this context, it is more appropriate than ever to offer young people a book that aims to present a reflection on life and evangelical virtues about which most adolescents have never heard. Carlo's life challenges us and is an invitation to discover or rediscover the gospel and God's love.

Very often, the young, who are too focused on themselves or the things of the world, look for an impossible happiness. They have never heard Jesus' invitation to follow Him or have not dared to talk to Him since their last children's prayer. Fr. Will Conquer uses accessible language and familiarizes them with Christ and His message. In selecting Carlo, a modern boy, who was one of their contemporaries, he has chosen an evangelical model who arouses both sympathy and admiration. He does not speak like a priest who preaches from the pulpit. Instead, he uses the communication tools of this new generation, the language of the social networks that fascinate and appeal to young people in every moment.

Carlo was a geek and a computer genius. But he was, above all, an authentic and sincere disciple and friend of Christ who, in his life, discovered a treasure that was greater than any other one. He bet his life on Jesus. The gospel and the Bible served him every day in navigating across the world's difficulties and dangers. The Eucharist and the Virgin Mary were his most precious loves. He would never have denied or abandoned them. We are talking about a boy of our time, and not some holy person who lived in a long-ago century. This is what makes Carlo both a person who is close to us and a model for new generations. I hope that this book will open up a place in the hearts of all those who are moving away from the Faith and no longer feel the need to believe.

Nicola Gori
Postulator for Carlo Acutis'
cause for canonization

Introduction

GOD'S HEROES

A world in crisis looks for heroes. God gives them some. We recently saw — on all of France's televisions — men and women who sacrificed their lives for a cause that surpassed them. We think of Lt. Col. Arnaud Beltrame and the soldiers who gave their lives for their brothers, so that everyone could live freely. We think of the firefighters who threw themselves into the Cathedral of Notre-Dame de Paris, when it caught on fire in 2019, to save our civilization's treasures. We think of John Bradburne, who spent his life near lepers in Zimbabwe until he died with them.

We hear about these daily heroes on television, in the newspapers, and on Facebook for a few weeks. But their witness, in the end, is rapidly drowned out in the media frenzy of successful shows or political fights of the moment. And yet, their actions have had a considerable impact. Their lives, like Carlo's life, reveal to us that we must be anchored in reality. Our challenge with this book is, therefore, precisely this — to become realistic. It is to offer you—the young and the not-as-young—what Jesus offered St. Matthew when he caught his eye 2,000 years ago in Galilee: "Follow me" (Matt. 9:9).

Nobody represented this call better than the painter Caravaggio in a series of three paintings that are found in France's national church in Rome—the Church of Saint Louis of the French. This triptych illustrates the call of a publican who shook up the social conventions of his time and changed history when he became an apostle of Christ. A detail in this first painting immediately strikes us. Christ is shown, along with Saint Peter, in a tunic, the historical garb of their time. In contrast, Matthew, along with the four men who surround him, are dressed like the Pontifical Swiss Guard—in Renaissance clothes—at the time this picture was painted. This portrayal teaches us that if Christ's call is really that of the historical Jesus, who died and rose again 2,000 years ago in Jerusalem, it also meets us where we are, in time and space. Today, we have to paint a new painting of Matthew's call, a painting that calls out to each one of us. The clothes of the characters who are depicted must show us that the holiness to which Jesus calls us does not remain frozen 2,000 years ago in a picture that was painted 400 years ago. These clothes must tell us that holiness is not fictional, but that it has to incarnate itself in our reality. Today, the world needs saints in jeans and tennis shoes.

In each generation, God has not stopped creating new models of holiness. We could write the history of the Church through these figures—from Jesus, to the first apostles, to the first Christian martyrs, to the first missionaries, to the first monasteries, to the great saints of the Middle Ages, to the reformers who put the poor back into the heart of the Church, to the explorers who carried the good news to the New World, and to the heroes who resisted the extremism of the twentieth century. In this whole array of saints, I am thinking especially of those great figures who did not wait for years to choose holiness. St. Joan of Arc was, in fact, only a young adolescent when she brought the king back on France's throne. During the Renaissance, St. Aloysius Gonzaga did not even have time to finish his novitiate. Later, in the industrial era, St. Dominic Savio, St. John Bosco's student, died before leaving the playground. What will be our model for the twenty-first century? Can God still offer us an itinerary of holiness in a world that seems so disoriented to us?

THREE LITTLE PIGS
AND NEW FOUNDATIONS

In the depth of his heart, every human being wants to be happy. But nobody really knows how to build a "house of happiness." To build a physical house, we start by thinking, dreaming about a beautiful project, and learning the rules of construction. To build a good life, we should act similarly. Rather than rushing into our endeavor blindly, without really knowing what to do, we should stop and ask ourselves, in the depths of our hearts, what we want in life and how we can attain it. If we want to be happy, and to be eternally happy, only an eternal God who truly loves us will be able to satisfy the desires of our hearts. It couldn't be any better. He directs us. His house is the one we need to build in our lives. In the story of the Three Little Pigs, which was made famous all around the world when it was adapted by the Disney Studios in 1933, we easily find this image in seeing that only the solid house resists the Big Bad Wolf's breath. Fifer Pig's straw house is blown away. Fiddler Pig's wooden house does not hold up either. Practical Pig builds his house with bricks. This house resists. But what the story does not tell us is that even a solid house can fall apart over time. On the one hand, our dear Practical Pig relies only on his own strength. On the other hand, the Big Bad Wolf in real life, the devil, does not run away forever deep into the woods. Little pigs aside, there is only one foundation that can last forever. You've guessed it. It is Matthew's — the Gospel of Matthew, chapter 9, verse 9. Matthew's house is still standing. He became a pillar of the Church because he built his house on the eternal rock by responding to Christ's call: "Follow me."[1] It is the same for us. We must give our lives solid foundations to resist today's winds of temptation that want to drag us away. Jesus is this foundation.

---

1. "As Jesus passed on from there, he saw a man called Matthew sitting at the tax office; and he said to him, 'Follow me.' And he rose and followed him" (Matt. 9:9).

Therefore, we must construct a house that is well-built. The frame of a solid life is the structure of virtue. Virtue is almost scary — like something that would transform us into a bronze statue. In reality, in a world without virtues, life is unbearable, as in a yard of hyenas. But if virtue is only a list of precepts and rules for good behavior, we risk becoming a society of robots who are programmed to live together without harming each other too much. This is a society in which everyone lives his own little life according to a bourgeois morality that does not make waves. What a hell!

CANONS OF HOLINESS

What can the Christian Faith add to virtue? When the Church recognizes a person's exceptional life, we get a good idea about what is possible. In the Catholic Church, the process for being recognized as a saint is a rather long one. It leads to canonization, which is an official and definitive declaration by the pope, most often from St. Peter's Square in Vatican City. Canonization is like recognizing a "knockout," i.e., a stunning girl or guy, a model of physical beauty. In the case of canonization, it is a spiritual beauty, that is to say, a beauty of virtue and holiness. At the very beginning of this process, a candidate is first recognized as a "Servant of God." This recognition follows a rather unique decree which, at this stage, is not authenticating any reported miracle or inviting special devotion to the candidate under consideration. After a meticulous study of the file containing a whole series of documents on the person's life, the Church's Congregation for the Causes of Saints recognizes they lived a life of heroic virtue.[2] On the basis of this decree, the person is then said to be "Venerable." Next comes beatification,[3] for which the Church typically requires an initial miracle, and then, usually following the approval of a second miracle, canonization. These last two stages take place after the Venerable is asked to intercede before God on behalf of the Christian faithful.

Before even recognizing these miracles, the person's heroic character must be proven. It is heroic not because he has done great things, triumphed on the battlefield, or won the Nobel Peace Prize, but because of his virtues. We often mistakenly imagine that the great saints accomplished great miracles, achieved extraordinary works, or changed the history of the world. Above all, saints are men and women who were heroes of virtue that can be role models for our lives today.

---

2. In each process of canonization, a specific person is even designated to emphasize all the difficulties of the case that is being studied and to say out loud what the world is softly telling itself. This is what is called the "devil's advocate." He is charged with asking all the bothersome questions and, in particular, to shine a light on each doubt that we could have.
3. This was the case with Carlo Acutis, who was proclaimed a blessed by the Church after a miraculous healing was attributed to his intercession.

THE COMPASS OF VIRTUES

So, what are their recognized virtues? Almost everyone has already heard about the seven deadly sins. But who knows that there are, above all, seven crucial virtues to live a good life? There are, first of all, four virtues, which are like the main points of a compass. They are called the cardinal virtues: justice, prudence, fortitude, and temperance. These four virtues, which can be compared to the four walls of a house, fit together perfectly with the three theological virtues that Jesus revealed and gives to each of his disciples, beginning at Baptism: faith, hope, and charity (i.e., love). The theological virtues are like the dome that crowns a church. The cardinal virtues enable a man to live a life of integrity but are not enough to make one a true Christian. They are, by themselves, like a house without a roof. We all have these virtues, to one extent or another. But nobody can live them heroically without God's help.

Christ is the perfect model of all these virtues. He is our model of justice when He defends the poor and gives back to everyone what he deserves. He is our model of prudence, for He always acts reasonably. He is our model of fortitude, for He has the courage to triumph over His enemies until He triumphs over death and Hell. He is our model of temperance because, although He is omnipotent, He becomes the servant. Jesus is our model in every virtue, for He is God, and God is love. God's love transforms our own virtues, and all our small endeavors. Without this love of God, and without His charity and grace, all our attempts to become holy are in vain. To be Christian is, therefore, to imitate Christ in His virtues, especially in His love for God and the world. Each chapter of this book is associated with a particular virtue, first of all, to understand how Carlo Acutis was able to practice them in a holy way, but, above all, to examine our own everyday lives and see how we're living them—and how we can live them better.

CARLO, OUR LITTLE HERO

In each generation, heroes of the faith, whom the Church recognizes as saints, emerge. They have understood that holiness is not about imagining past holiness or dreaming about a better world; rather, it is living their present lives as disciples of Christ. Therefore, holiness takes place in the here and now. Everybody is called to embrace his own unique call to holiness that God gives him. Of course, we are not saying that it is easy. On the contrary, we are saying that it is heroic. However, this holiness is not inaccessible. These heroes are not always those we think about. In reality, they are not all that different from us. This book will actually make us discover a hero who resembles us.

Carlo Acutis could be the first millennial to become a saint.[4] Thus, he would be the first twenty-first century

---

4. Millennials, who are also called Generation Y, are characterized as being born in the '80s and '90s and, therefore, growing up with new technologies, including social media.

adolescent to be offered to us as a model by the Church, the first young person of the third millennium to be cited by a pope, and the first saint to be recognized by the Church in a context that it is common to us. He grew up in the Europe that we know—a peaceful Europe that we can freely travel in. He would be the first saint to enter Heaven with a cellphone in his hand, to have used a computer, sent emails, done research on Google, and found answers to his questions there. From the time he was a child until he was fifteen years old, he was confronted by the same problems we have personally encountered. Through the research that I have done to write this spiritual biography, I have really been touched by him. Carlo is one of my direct contemporaries. We have experienced the same historical events and shared a number of common challenges in our relationship with God and others. His life has opened my eyes to many chapters of my adolescence that I would prefer to leave in the unexamined drawers of my past. He has reconciled me with it. By immersing yourself, in turn, in his life, you will notice how much he looks like us more and more.

Of course, there is perhaps something that differentiates us. He could already be in Heaven. We are still here on earth. But do we have to be dead in order to be holy? This is the first question we can ask ourselves when we see the faces of our immortalized saints, whether it be through white marble sculptures, Renaissance paintings, or black-and-white photos for the most contemporary ones. We see that Carlo was really alive and very colorful. He smiled at life and played different sports, ranging from soccer to skiing. He loved computer science. He ran everywhere, traveled to the four corners of Europe, and, in every situation, maintained a good sense of humor and was quick-witted. Even in Heaven, Carlo continues to be very much alive—indeed, even more than ever! Like St. Thérèse of Lisieux, he can repeat: "I will spend my heaven doing good on earth." Today, his reputation has spread to five continents. Facebook pages from Australia to Korea are dedicated to him. His life is already inspiring the themes of musicals in France. The official site[5] that is devoted to him is now available in six languages, including Chinese! This devotion extends to Brazil. Many people suffering from serious illnesses have asked God to have the faith that Carlo had in facing his illness—the deadly leukemia that struck him. Many have even been healed and attribute their healing directly to Carlo's specific intercession for them![6] Finally, websites that Carlo developed to evangelize are still functioning, and are seen and accessed by many users. The exhibitions on Eucharistic miracles he created continue to go around in many churches.

---

5. www.carloacutis.com.
6. Doctors commissioned by the Congregation for the Causes of Saints meticulously study cases of unexplained healings with very precise criteria. One reported miracle attributed to Carlo's intercession met those criteria, leading to his October 2020 beatification.

On their own, the dead cannot do anything good for those of us on earth. But if Carlo continues to do so much good—and touch so many hearts who, by his witness, return to God and the Church—he is truly alive and close to God.

HOLINESS AS A LIFE PROGRAM

Nonetheless, we do not become heroes simply by changing costume like cinematic superheroes do. Heroism is not learned in one night. We have to live in order to acquire all the virtues we need in today's world. Carlo made use of his whole life to live out these virtues. Creating a masterpiece takes time—sometimes several years. The same thing applies to a masterpiece of holiness. But be warned! Holiness is not the absence of sin. If that were the case, it would be better for us not to have been born, for each day that goes by would be a dreaded opportunity to fall. Holiness is not a black-and-white, spotless painting[7] like Kazimir Malevich's black square, but a life that is totally filled with God's grace. It is a painting with a thousand colors, like the angel wings on Fra Angelico's frescoes. To become a saint at the age of fifteen is to succeed in what most of us have not yet managed to do when we are twenty, thirty, or even ninety-nine. Our own life, if we look at it with a certain amount of honesty and humility, should remind us that what Carlo experienced is not all that ordinary. With all the trials of life, the

---

7. The Blessed Mother is a notable exception.

simple fact of remaining faithful and joyful in adolescence is a challenge for most of us.

But to recognize Carlo's holiness is also to accept, along with him, the challenge that the holiness he took up in our world is indeed attainable. Carlo was not more predisposed to be holy than we are. All of us have been called to be holy since the day of our Baptism. Holiness is not just good behavior and good manners that our parents could teach us. It is an authentic and personal encounter that Carlo's life will show us. His life exuded authenticity. It was not a life that was invented or embellished like a blissful legend. The testimonies of holiness that are as fresh as Carlo's are rare. Even rarer are the saints about whom we can still question so many living witnesses. You just have to walk around the streets of Assisi with Carlo's mother to be aware of it today. Everyone wants to talk to tell her about a memory shared with her son.

All these testimonies have been gathered, piece by piece, into an immense file, the positio, which has been compiled by Nicola Gori, the postulator, the one whose mission is to make Carlo known to the Church and the world. The life of Carlo that you will read about here is, therefore, neither a historical novel nor an imaginary tale. It is neither Harry Potter nor The Little Prince. But it is perhaps better. It is a young person, like you and me, who wants to share with us the joy of already being in Heaven.

Chapter 1
The Child Who Knocked Down Walls

CHRISTMAS 1991

 This was Carlo Acutis' first Christmas. A year the world experienced enormous disruption. For almost 50 years, the planet had been divided into two blocs: On the one hand, there was the Western Bloc, including the United States, Great Britain, France, and Italy. On the other hand, there was the Eastern Bloc, including the Union of Soviet Socialist Republics, which was called the U.S.S.R., East Germany, Poland, Czechoslovakia, and Hungary. The political ideologies and visions of each side led to confrontation. This confrontation was so extreme that it almost dragged the entire world into a third World War.

But in December 1991, a page was being turned. In a historical speech that was broadcast on television, Mikhail Gorbachev officially resigned from his position as president of the Soviet Union. The red flag no longer waved over the Kremlin. The Cold War ended, two years after the fall of the Berlin Wall: the wall that had separated the world for decades. Communism's promises, that boasted of a model of paradise on earth, had gone out the window and left a bitter taste for the populations that experienced its harsh regime. The conquest of airspace, which the United States and Soviet Union had undertaken as an ultimate means of subduing each other with weapons systems, was cut short.

In December 1991, the "race to the stars" was forced to a halt in front of the Christmas star. For a long time, voices had made themselves heard on bringing down Communist barriers. Some figures, like Russian dissident Alexander Solzhenitsyn, who knew firsthand the gulag (concentration camps in Siberia), and Pope John Paul II, who was elected in 1979, spared no effort to free the people confined behind Communist walls of hate. Gorbachev said, "Nothing that happened in Eastern Europe would have been possible without the Pope's presence." Men were needed to tear down these walls. These were men who did not derive their strength from the power of weapons, but from the power of faith.

A world was dying, and a new one, whose dawn glimmered on the horizon, was being born. The upheavals that were generated are such that this period can seem distant to us. Yet, it is in this changing time that our story begins.

A RAY OF SUNSHINE IN GRAY LONDON

Like nearly 25,000 expatriated Italians in London, Carlo's future parents came to the city for their work. Antonia Salzano was twenty-four, and Andrea Acutis was twenty-six. They hoped to start their careers abroad in a global financial advisory and asset management group. They naturally chose this city, prized by many Italians, but also strategic in their line of business. Far from their family and homeland, Andrea and Antonia, who were married in 1990, enjoyed the advantages and challenges of a city that was both vibrant and stressful. The couple enjoyed the hectic life in London, where they could easily find their friends after long workdays, drink a pint in the pub to relax, visit museums, travel without pressure, and simply spend time with each other.

A few months after their wedding, so far from home, Antonia was pleasantly surprised to discover she was pregnant. The couple had to arrange for the things they needed in order to welcome their first child—a baby carriage, clothes, a crib, etc. We can imagine this time—full of the emotions associated with the arrival of a newborn—must not have been easy, especially because of the difference in language and culture. Separation from family members in Italy must have added stress, for their family could only provide prenatal support from a distance.

Carlo Acutis was born on May 3, 1991. (If his birth on earth was similar to that of an exile's, his birth unto eternal life is already a happier event that unites his whole family.) Fifteen days after his birth, Carlo was baptized in Our Lady of Sorrows Church in London. This church is dedicated to Our Lady of Fatima, the pilgrimage site in Portugal, where Carlo would visit years later as a pilgrim. Even his great-grandmother Adriana traveled from Italy to celebrate this powerful moment and offer him her baptismal medal. Carlo's grandparents were so happy to be there that the parents chose his paternal grandfather, Carlo, to be godfather and his maternal grandmother, Luana, to be the little child's godmother. Family is sacred to Italians!

On the day of his Baptism, Carlo's mother Antonia made a traditional cake in the shape of a lamb, symbolically evoking the purpose of this child's Baptism. The lamb recalls the moment when Abraham sought to sacrifice his son Isaac, in obedience to God. But the angel held his hand back, providing him a ram as a sacrificial substitute. The cake's shape is also reminiscent of the Passover lambs, whose blood the Hebrews used to mark their doors to protect them from the scourge that struck Egypt. Most of all, though, it recalls Jesus Christ, of whom John the Baptist said, "Behold, the Lamb of God, who takes away the sin of the world!" (John 1:29). In fact, this connection to Christ reminds us that Carlo's Baptism was not merely an occasion for the family to gorge themselves on petits fours (small cakes), but a celebration of God's eternal love for this child. For many months now, Carlo's parents had desired, hoped for, and loved him. But from all eternity, God had wanted to save Carlo, as He wants to save all of His children.

All of the difficulties of business and financial life found in the city made Carlo's parents miss the Italian sun. Little Carlo's arrival brought light to his parents' life, a ray of sunshine in the midst of London's gray skies. A child's arrival is always a joyful moment. Carlo was lucky to be born in a family that loved him and plied him with affection. His little eyes moved about his home, as if he were already trying to understand the world around him. In time, his curiosity would grow and spur him on to become interested in his Christian Faith, the study of other religions, computer science, painting, movies, and zoology. His parents spent hours watching him sleep, play, and wonder at the world. They themselves wondered: What would he become? What would he look like when he was older? Would he be happy in life? For the time being, they gave him the best they had. This included making all the sacrifices associated with raising a child, including waking at night to calm Carlo's tears, and having their pace of life disrupted by the addition of a third person. Carlo's new life also consisted of the heavenly life that his Baptism opened him up to.

Carlo's first word was one shared with many little children: "Daddy." Soon after, he also said "Mommy." Grateful parents know a child is worth more than all the gold in the world. Carlo's parents discovered their infant son's vulnerability—and their own fears—when they hired a young nanny to care for Carlo when his mother started working again.

His first nanny, a young Scottish woman, did a good job of looking after Carlo, despite some mishaps. One evening, Carlo smelled of alcohol, the way a drunken elderly man does. The baby was a little young for booze, wasn't he? After questioning his nanny, they understood her unusual methods: "A little alcohol in something like liquid Tylenol could help children sleep." Another time, when coming back home, they found the nanny asleep on the sofa next to Carlo, with what seemed to be dry blood on both of them. Several scenarios flashed to mind. Did Carlo spit out blood during his sleep? Was he wounded? Thankfully, the nanny allayed their fears. She had a guilty pleasure: chocolate bars. This time, though, she fell asleep before putting away her unfinished candy, and the chocolate melted and stained the clothes of both nanny and child. What a relief!

The Acutis family had only this brief London experience abroad, for they returned to Italy shortly after Carlo's birth to work in their families' respective businesses. Andrea Acutis took over the family business that his father, Carlo Acutis Sr. had developed as the main stakeholder in Italy's insurance market. This position offered a privileged financial situation for the Acutis family. Antonia would work in the publishing company run by her family. Carlo and his parents left London in September 1991, accompanied by a new young Irish nanny. This was her first trip outside the British Isles, and she arrived in Italy—the land of spaghetti, pizza, and serenades—with various fears. She worried about everything regarding little Carlo and surprised his parents by refusing to drink water from the faucet, "because it was Italian water and probably not very good."

Later, when Carlo went to the daycare center, a new Polish nanny grew annoyed when she saw Carlo hassled by the other children. She was misled by Carlo's mild temperament; she thought he was "too good" and wanted Carlo to defend himself. He needed to set boundaries with others, she believed, so as not have his toys taken away. But despite all her exhortations, she did not manage to make him more combative. One day, he replied: "But Jesus would not be happy if I lost my temper."

From an early age, Carlo had a natural ability to relate to others. He was passionate about meeting people. He was a spontaneous child, who did not hold back his loving outbursts, whether tenderly greeting his parents first thing in the morning or joyously saying hello to friends and strangers on the streets. Even adults who tended to be irritated by the presence of children let themselves be touched by this unusually pleasant and curious little boy.

VACATIONS
AT NONNA'S IN CENTOLA

Each summer, from May to September, Carlo was entrusted to his maternal grandparents, who welcomed him in the family home south of Naples, in the village of Centola, which is in the Province of Salerno. This small hilltop village dominates Cape Palinuro and the coast of Cilento. It is a little-known jewel in southern Italy with a well-preserved coastline and a beautiful national park that is especially known for its orchids. The villages seem to be frozen in the past. Carlo's great-grandparents had met there. His maternal great-grandmother, who was born in the United States in New York, came from a family of landowners. Because of her generosity in difficult financial times, the sailors in Naples and Salerno fondly remembered her. At the beginning of the twentieth century, in fact, many Neapolitans lived in poverty and were driven into exile in France, Belgium, and the United States. This occurred after a serious agricultural crisis that following Italy's unification by Italian Republicans. Carlo's great-grandmother's generosity toward the poor was such that we still find old black-and-white photos of her among the coastal fishermen. This coast is like a set from a movie. Its innumerable caves and old churches offered many places for Carlo to explore.

During one of these vacations, when he was only five, Carlo's young Polish nanny took him to the Shrine of the Blessed Virgin of the Holy Rosary in Pompeii, one of Italy's biggest churches. (Pompeii is also, of course, the city Mount Vesuvius destroyed when it erupted in A.D. 79.) For Carlo's young nanny, this visit to the Shrine was decisive in increasing her faith and devotion. She had grown up on the other side of the Iron Curtain in Communist Poland, so going to a church to pray in her homeland was forbidden or strictly controlled. Here in Italy, she enjoyed the happiness to pray freely and allow herself to be touched by Carlo's already luminous faith. Carlo loved the Blessed Mother, whom he considered his Mother, with all his heart.

During these summers spent in southern Italy, Carlo experienced both an adventurous and innocent childhood. In the morning, he would go to Centola's downtown market with his grandmother. Later in the afternoon, he would travel to the beach, where his grandparents treated him to a snack, which included *paninis* (sandwiches) and fruits. His grandfather's garden had a lovely variety of fruit trees, and Carlo liked to gather their bounty, including wild berries, figs, and pomegranates. The harvest was so good Carlo's grandfather often had enough to offer his neighbors. In exchange, the neighbors gave Carlo's grandfather fruits grown at their homes, as well as chicken eggs. By communing with nature amid this rustic calm, Carlo was free to let his imagination and childhood dreams expand. He breathed a simple atmosphere there, which was rich in humanity and surely contributed to the development of his open and lively temperament. He had a way of being both gentle and authentic, which made him very likeable to all the village's inhabitants. The region's people appreciated his unusual kindness and goodwill. Carlo was the son of a good family, who arrived from northern Italy, to spend his vacations in the south. However, he was not one of the local *pinzuti*, as Corsicans describe Parisians who vacation in Corsica during the summer. They saw him as one of their own, since his presence communicated so much joy. His gregarious personality enabled him to make friends quickly with everyone. One summer, his grandmother, Luana, was invited to celebrate a village friend's seventieth birthday. She suggested that Carlo, who was twelve at the time, come with her, so as not to leave him alone in the house. To her great surprise, her grandson fit in well with all the village elders at the birthday party. They were all piqued by this young man who, though only a child, demonstrated a rare open-mindedness and maturity.

What most surprised the old ladies of the village was everyday seeing Carlo in church. After spending afternoons at the beach, he joined the devout women who faithfully prayed the Rosary in a way that was sometimes mechanical. His presence positively challenged them, helping restore a real enthusiasm to their prayer. In addition, during Mass, gossip ceased out of deference to Carlo's silence and meditation. In a village where everyone knew each other, Carlo's smile and presence renewed the atmosphere, which was often full of solitude. We might think such behavior should be expected from a child whose parents sought to provide him the best possible education. But there was more than that to Carlo, because there are some things you cannot teach or force someone to learn, such as the kindness Carlo showed toward everyone. He was selfless, and his ready smile brought happiness to those he encountered.

THE PROPERTY CARETAKERS' GUARDIAN ANGEL

When Carlo was old enough for grade school, his parents chose one of Milan's most elite schools. However, because it was too far from their home, Carlo's parents switched their son to a nearby school after only three months. Change is never easy for young people, and even more so changing schools mid-year. Carlo had hardly met his first friends when he had to leave them. But he was very warmly welcomed by young nuns at his new school—Sister Andreina and Sister Marcellina. They had given their lives to care for children, and so Carlo's abrupt change was made less painful by their maternal presence. These nuns lived out their vocation with affection and tenderness. And they still remember the little six-year-old who smiled at them every morning.

Carlo's daily walks from home to school were an opportunity for surprising encounters . . . with property caretakers. Each day, Carlo crossed paths with many of them, shouting "*buon giorno!*" with his cheerful, childhood voice and a smile. Most of these caretakers were surprised that this young, privileged boy was so friendly to them. He would stop to speak to each of them learn their names, and then thereafter greet them personally. In most cases, these caretakers were not Italians, and they felt a wall between them and the affluent people who lived in the buildings whose security they maintained. Their living quarters at these properties almost became a prison when relationships with the owners became tense.

As people who resided on the first floor, the caretakers were very different from the Milanese elite who lived and rubbed shoulders with each other on the upper floors. But Carlo did not make any class distinctions. Years later, a property caretaker on the Via Ariosto would tell Carlo's parents how much their son's kindness touched him. This man, who had only been in Italy for a short while and probably did not know the local language well, had been feeling rather inferior in his new surroundings. He said young Carlo's daily acts of charity were a real source of comfort for him during this difficult time in his life. The caretaker of the building where Carlo grew up gave similar testimony. This little Italian's genuine spirit offered serenity to anyone who met him. You just had to spend a little time with him to see life with more hope. Carlo made people feel valued regardless of their origin or state in life. He immediately made people feel at ease because of the consideration he showed when he met them. Perhaps Carlo was too young to be aware of the weight of social and cultural differences. Or perhaps his heart was sufficiently pure and simple to understand that these differences were not so important.

Carlo impacted many others in his short life, including not only guardians of properties but guardians of faith. The young child was not intimidated by anything or anyone. His parents had many priest friends who came to dinner at the Acutis home, and who left edified by having met Carlo. One such family friend was a priest in charge of the Church's Congregation for the Doctrine of the Faith. He had come to spend the day with them in Assisi. Sometimes Church leaders can seem distant, unreachable, and barricaded behind doctrinal walls. But young Carlo did not let ecclesiastical status cow him. He dared to ask the priest questions. This Roman prelate still recalls the positive impression Carlo, when only an adolescent, made on him. Carlo had a lively and well-formed faith, which he sought to deepen. In addition, Carlo was not afraid share his plans and dreams with strangers, including an erudite Jesuit priest and professor at both the Pontifical Oriental Institute and the Pontifical Biblical Institute. (The Acutis family supported these two schools with scholarships for underprivileged students.) This Jesuit was surprised by Carlo's candor. He was used to academic conversations, so Carlo's simple questions about the Gospels unsettled him. Unlike others, Carlo did not dwell on the priest's diplomas. Carlo simply wanted to know who Jesus was for this cleric and what the Bible really proclaimed. The meeting with young Carlo would leave an indelible mark on the professor's faith and how he lived his priesthood.

This is also what a Little Sister of Jesus said. Carlo would have many discussions with her. This sister had much experience dialoguing with believers of other faiths. Carlo liked to ask her questions about the years she spent in India. His simple questions broke down the age barriers between him and the elderly nun. They spent a lot of time talking. How do we best serve Jesus? Do we do it by becoming a missionary on the other side of the world, by taking care of the poor and bringing God's love to them? Or do we do it by staying where God has put us and praying for all those who need our support? The elderly nun explained that the two can go together. It was, in any case, how she hoped to live. A few years later, she understood the mission Carlo had received and embraced — that of letting himself be plucked like a flower from God's garden and going to pray for her in Heaven. During the last week of his life, Carlo would tell her, "I offer all that for you." He opened her eyes to the power of intercessory prayer, in which we ask God to come to the aid of a brother or sister. Such prayer enables us to surmount all boundaries, even the one that separates Heaven and earth. The nun said she was sure Heaven was where Carlo was doing his volunteer work now.

RAJESH

Young Carlo did not need to go to the other side of the world to serve his neighbor. Yet, we can wonder how a child served so many in his short life. How and why would a child venture outside his privileged and protective environment? Was it not enough for him to play quietly in his room and dream of a better world like all of the world's other children? How was he mature enough to open himself up to precarious situations outside his privileged bubble? His conversations did not simply consist of sweet words and comfortable emotions. It is never so easy to convert our good words into actions. But Carlo's words were not simply words.... While it is true that Carlo was blessed to be born into a very well-to-do family, he often thought of other children who did not have the same advantages. They did not learn to read or write and make friends at school, but instead were exploited in factories. Compared to them, Carlo was very lucky. But he was not satisfied with prayerfully entrusting such people to the good Lord. He also knew how to open his eyes.

Among the people in his parents' service, Carlo noticed one who had worked for several years with a touching humility and fidelity. Rajesh took care of the Acutises' daily tasks. He was Indian[8] and left his country, family,

---

8. Rajesh grew up on the island of Mauritius and did his graduate studies in India.

and friends to seek a new fortune in Italy. He was born in a family that was poor but conscious of its dignity. In fact, Rajesh's father and mother belonged to the Brahman caste, the highest caste—or social class—in Hindu society. His parents gave him a popular name. It still is today in India. It is the name of the actor Rajesh Khanna, the first superstar in Bollywood, India's Hollywood. Perhaps this name might bring Rajesh his own happiness? When he arrived in Italy, Rajesh became completely homesick.

India is a big country that enjoys a thousand-year-old civilization. But it is also a country wounded by fratricidal wars between Hindus and Muslims, which have wrought bloody havoc on the nation. It has also been wounded by a caste system that legitimizes inequalities and the rejection of the lowest and most scorned castes, known as the "untouchables." But India is even more wounded by poverty. This poverty would touch Mother Teresa's heart on the streets of Calcutta. She would fight against it all her life. Once in Italy, Rajesh was very far from all these problems. But his situation was turned upside down. He who belonged to the Brahman caste, found himself a servant. He who was rich in a poor country, became poor in a rich country. People looked up to him at home, merely because of his birth. But here in Italy, people hardly looked at him, simply because of his work.

Yet there was one who was strong enough to look at him for who he really was. Carlo quickly formed a

friendship with Rajesh. As the years went by, this friendship would deepen. Carlo thought that Rajesh was not
a simple family employee, but a member of their household. Since they shared the same roof, they could also
share the same table. Carlo spoke to Rajesh about everything, from school and his friends, to his joys and sorrows,
his hopes and disappointments. Carlo also listened, for he
wanted to know everything about India, Rajesh's native
land, including its traditions and culture. Since Carlo
was very young, he had been fascinated by world cultures
and did not understand that they could be regarded with
contempt by others. One day, after leaving grade school,
some of Carlo's friends started to laugh at a group of
Indian mothers because they were dressed differently, i.e.,
because they wore saris.[9] Immediately, Carlo grew angry
and condemned the mockery. He loved the richness of
different cultures. But Rajesh was struck that this child
was not afraid to talk about what everyone else preferred
to keep silent. Carlo did not have the middle-class reserve
that many adults hide behind for fear of opening their
hearts to new people. Carlo talked about everything. He

---

9. The sari is a traditional item of clothing worn by millions of women in
southern Asia (mainly in India, Nepal, Bangladesh, Sri Lanka, Pakistan,
and Iran). Its origin goes back to 100 B.C. To live like the Indian women
with whom she rubbed shoulders, Mother Teresa and all the sisters of her
religious community, the Missionaries of Charity, would also wear saris.
Theirs is white, the color of Baptism, with three blue bands on the fringe,
as a reminder of the theological virtues of faith, hope, and charity.

believed that talking about everything inevitably meant talking about what was going on at the heart of his life. Indeed, Rajesh quickly understood that Carlo's friendship with Jesus was really at the center of all that he experienced and shared.

This was unnerving for Rajesh, who, up until now, had never met anyone who used such simple words to share his faith. Who was this Jesus really, for whom all these cities and villages in Europe erected churches, cathedrals, and basilicas? Churches and crosses filled Italian cities and landscapes. Nonetheless, nobody successfully shared the meaning of this heritage to Rajesh, this Indian domestic worker. But Carlo talked to him about Jesus without intentionally proselytizing him, as a friend talks about a friend to his friends. He shared everything about his spiritual discoveries with Rajesh, who marveled at the boy's enthusiasm.

As a little child, Carlo practiced reading to Rajesh the stories of famous saints—for example, St. Francis of Assisi and St. Joan of Arc. Then, once Carlo was at ease doing that, he began to read the Bible with his friend. Carlo was proud that he could finally show someone he knew his way around the Bible: "You see, that is the Old Testament. It is before Jesus. It is the biggest part of my Bible. And from there, it is called the New Testament, which tells the story of the life of Jesus and His disciples." Rajesh learned about it all from Carlo, who sincerely explained everything to him. While growing up, our young friend also discovered the *Catechism of the Catholic Church*,[10] and he played question-and-answer games with Rajesh. Little by little, Carlo evangelized his friend, for Rajesh could see that the boy was not simply curious but had a real inner strength that pushed him to live and share his faith. As the years went by, his conversations with Carlo became increasingly instructive, as Rajesh, an informal catechumen, learned all the fundamentals of the Christian Faith. The Brahman caste to which Rajesh's family belonged is India's priestly caste. This social origin had previously led Rajesh to ask himself about God's existence. Now his faith-related conversations with Carlo fascinated him. One day, Carlo dared to ask Rajesh if he thought he could become happier by drawing closer to Jesus. On Carlo's advice, Rajesh asked for Baptism.[11] Thus, through encountering Carlo, Rajesh became aware that the Christian Faith is not a label for the privileged, but a treasure to share with all.

Carlo's Catholic faith was so radiant that it spread to — and through — all those who encountered him because of the serenity and gentleness with which the boy shared the truths of the Faith. Rajesh even introduced his friend Seeven Kistnen to him. Carlo would talk to him about his

---

10. The compendium that summarizes the Catholic Church's teaching on faith and morals.

11. This story reflects one traditional story of a certain Clement, a servant in a Roman family a thousand years ago. After converting to Christianity, the one who was only a slave finally became the pope, Peter's third successor.

trips to Fatima and Lourdes and about the miracle of God's love in his life. Seeven would, in turn, ask for Baptism, while being eternally grateful to Carlo for having communicated this passion to him. Seeven said that he was touched by Carlo's Christian witness, including his great generosity and humility, which he had never seen anyone else exemplify. Carlo had an inner strength that enabled him to go beyond the boundaries of his life on earth. And it mattered not that Rajesh and Seeven did not have the same salary, skin color, or origin as his parents. Rajesh said:

> In light of the importance of faith in Carlo's life, it was natural for him to talk to me about it. He was very gifted in explaining concepts in simple words that even adults couldn't explain to me. Little by little, I started to take seriously the advice and the little catechism lessons that he gave me at the corner of a table—up until the day when I asked for Baptism.

Without any calculation or ulterior motives, Carlo let his love overflow. These two men, touched by Christ through Carlo's testimony, were grateful for his courage to share how God had loved them from all eternity.

THE QUIET STRENGTH

Despite his age, Carlo demonstrated courage in many of life's challenges—the courage to talk when others preferred to remain silent;

the courage to meet the one who was alone when others preferred to ignore him; and the courage to smile at life, when life was no longer smiling back. Strength is needed to knock down walls. It is paradoxical to talk about strength when we are speaking about a child. Carlo's strength was far from the strength we usually think of. His was not a brutal and destructive strength, but one that was free and well-considered. Carlo looked for what was good and desired what was just, precisely when that could seem difficult or even dangerous to us. Charles de Foucauld experienced this strength in the desert, just like Communism's resistance fighters who were deported to the gulags. Talking about one's faith is never without risks. It is, not coincidentally, the same virtue of the martyrs who, in laying down their lives for Jesus, performed the supreme act of courage and strength. Strength is both a virtue and a gift.

Carlo's strength of character was having the courage to meet others and daring to speak a word of reconciliation when opposing sides glared at each other. But this strength came from above when it allowed him to go further and testify about something that transcended him. David had this strength when he faced Goliath: he was the little shepherd who faced the most fearsome warrior, but he knew how to prevail, i.e., with God's help (1 Sam. 17:44–51). It is the strength that the Apostles received on the day of Pentecost, which enabled them to go throughout Jerusalem and to the ends of the earth to bear witness to the world about the Resurrection of Christ. This strength enabled Carlo to overcome his fears and continue to be resilient when facing obstacles, as when he had to separate himself from friends who were fighting. The strength of faith is not an attacking power, but an ability to resist wrongdoing. For, in the end, which one is the strongest—the terrorist who blows himself up like a desperate man—or an armed ship that holds back its ammunition so it can ensure peace? Courage gives us the strength to do the good for which we are aiming. All his life, Carlo had the courage to follow his convictions. For the world, the strength of a child may seem like nothing. It may seem like a little flower at the end of a rifle, or a white flag lost in battle. But, as Christians, we must recall that Carlo's model of strength was Jesus. Jesus was not someone who imposed Himself with the strength of his arms but somebody who spoke through bearing the weight of His Cross. Jesus had always done what was fair, even when it cost Him His life. Exercising courage is a virtue. But it brings us a deep peace when we know we have made the right decisions. This strength entails defending the truth and being kind, especially in difficult situations. It is the strength Carlo had in not cheating in school when the opportunity arose. It is not the strength of the bullies who mocked the weakest ones in their class, but the strength of the one who did not participate in their ridiculous games and took the side of those being ridiculed. It is the strength of the young adolescent who knows how to respect girls, without wanting to monopolize them. Carlo's strength was that of a young man who let God's grace work in him and who, while he was weak, allowed His strength to shine in himself.

An angelic authenticity emanated from his face. Carlo had this little smile, which was both good and naïve, like we find on the famous "Smiling Angel" on the facade of the Reims Cathedral in France. It was a smile that looked at the earth, but which seemed to see Heaven already. This was perhaps the biggest wall he knocked down. The wall of hatred that separates man from God became the avenue of divine love, which disarms the most withdrawn hearts. Carlo's loving smile knocked down walls. He built a bridge between earth and Heaven, from where he continues to smile at us today.

THE WORD OF GOD

But now in Christ Jesus you who once were far off have been brought near in the blood of Christ. For he is our peace, who has made us both one, and has broken down the dividing wall of hostility, by abolishing in his flesh the law of commandments and ordinances, that he might create in himself one new man in place of the two, so making peace, and might reconcile us both to God in one body through the cross, thereby bringing the hostility to an end.

And he came and preached peace to you who were far off and peace to those who were near; for through him we both have access in one Spirit to the Father. So then you are no longer strangers and sojourners, but you are fellow citizens with the saints and members of the household of God, built upon the foundation of the apostles and prophets, Christ Jesus himself being the cornerstone. (Eph. 2:13–20)

LIFE QUESTIONS

➤ In what way do the media, especially via the Internet, weaken me and prevent me from being my best self? Do I allow them to keep me away from Christ, or do I use them to get closer to Him?

➤ Do we need courage to resist pressure?

➤ What does it mean to have principles? Am I ready to take risks for what I believe in and for the One who believes in me?

➤ What prevents people from taking a position against something that, according to them, is not going well?

➤ Do I also let myself be carried away by the crowd of those who think the same way, or do I have the courage to be the person who I am?

PRAYER TO GOD

Almighty God, help me to do the right thing at all times without worrying what others say or think. Teach me to face my fears, knowing You are at my side. May I honestly try to be the best I can be every day. I know that I am not always courageous. But with Your gift of strength, let me always be available to try new things in faithfully following Jesus, Your Son, my model of courage.

Chapter 2
The Brother's Hope

THE WAR OF BROTHERS

Suddenly, everything went away. We thought that it was the end of the story. We thought that everything had been said. But then, once again, we learn that tragedy is not over. Our little Carlo grew in wisdom and intelligence. His life seemed to unfold like a long, calm river or painting without shadow. Of course, it was much less boring than an old 1980s film because Carlo was full of life, and his life was filled with vibrant encounters. But, in the end, it was seemingly calm. We could end with this picture of Carlo as handsome and nice. This was the little boy the whole world wanted. But is that holiness? The end would tell us that Carlo's life was a comedy, not a tragedy. His holiness was not that of Epinal's[12] paintings and plaster statues. Carlo was a real child, yet unlike others his age. At the same time,

---

12. Epinal is a town in France.

he lived in the same world we do. He could not flee this world and what is hardest and most revolting within it. The world knew an apparent tranquility after the end of the Cold War, which coincided with the year of Carlo's birth. That tranquility was echoed in Carlo's childhood, which we can contemplate by hanging onto the paradise of his youthful innocence. That would be a scene similar to the amazed magi and shepherds who contemplated the Christ Child. Yet, the pages in history turn, and history does not permit us to be ignorant of what happens after. After Bethlehem's peace, a cry was heard in the Ramah Valley. This cry was the Massacre of the Innocents—the massacre of the children and their mothers' cries.

We dream of a peace that lasts forever and holiness that is a child's game. But life teaches us the opposite, and it teaches us the hard way. Carlo did not believe that being holy was turning a blind eye to difficult situations, and God knows that he would see them! Carlo was only three years old in 1994. Horror could be seen while channel surfing on television, in between cartoons and informercials. The Trojan War was going on, but this time it was worse. It was almost unthinkable. Above all, one could not talk to children about it. It was a war between brothers, neighbors, and friends who visited each other in schools and church on one day, and who, grappled and killed each other on the next. It was a deadly civil war that took place in Rwanda. It was a war we thought we would never see again because of the

end of trench and bayonet warfare. It was a machine war.
Brothers killed each other with weapon in hand. Innocent
people were massacred and assassinated at point blank range.
This war knew no decency or limits. Even churches, which
usually serve as asylum, were violated as guerillas entered in
the middle of Mass to open fire on innocent victims whose
only mistake was belonging to a different ethnic group. It
was a war between Tutsis and Hutus, which occurred thousands of miles from Milan. And yet everyone witnessed it,
helplessly, behind his television set.

Carlo became a model of holiness in this world. God
also calls us to be in this world.

TO ENTER INTO TIME

Carlo would never have a brother or sister
during his lifetime.[13] He had no sibling with
whom he could play, eat his daily meals, argue,
or work through difficulties. Nor was there
anyone at home with whom he could otherwise
extend his childhood, whether in endless imaginary stories
combining firefighter trucks with plastic knights, or in a
beetle hunt under the sun of an Italian public garden. Carlo
would be an only child, irreversibly immersed in a world
of adults. This may have also contributed to his maturity

---

13. Four years after Carlo's death, his parents experienced the joy of having
twins—a girl and a boy, Francesca and Michele.

and precocious questioning. So, Carlo found himself alone
in the world. Except for a few visits at the daycare center,
a nanny took care of him at home up until he went to
school. Leaving the world of childhood and entering the
real world has its challenges. In a world of brutes, showing
tenderness becomes heroic. When everyone is fighting, it
is so easy to be caught up in fear, anxiety, or anger. People
want to fight back or suddenly flee. Carlo was not an angel
from Heaven. He was a boy like everyone, who was subject
to the same temptations.

It is not easy to know how Carlo went from this childhood innocence to what we call the age of reason — from
the age when we believe in Santa Claus and well-wrapped
gifts to the age when we confess our faith in the Heavenly
Father and His most beautiful gift, His Only Son, whom
He gave us and who was crucified on the Cross to save
us. When we are only a little child, everything seems so
simple. Faith is a foregone conclusion. Our parents say
this or that to us. We learn in catechism that, of course,
God is alive! When Carlo was a child, he believed that
God was alive in this simple way, from the first babblings
in the cradle; the sweet prayers hummed by his mother;
and through the Rosaries that he devoutly prayed with the
elderly ladies of his grandparents' village. When do we ask
ourselves for the first time if God really exists? At what
age do we ask ourselves if God hears us and makes Himself
present, or if it is all simply a child's fable? There must be

an age or even a day when we start asking ourselves all of these questions.

It is not easy to know when Carlo experienced this day. Unlike his female friends, Carlo did not keep an intimate diary. Thus, we do not have a written record of the deep yearnings of his heart, unlike St. Thérèse, who left us, a century earlier, with the diary called *Story of a Soul*. Thus, we will never know about his first crush, the first time he pilfered a snack, or the sadness and struggles in his heart.

What *Story of a Soul* shows us about little Thérèse is that some of her first questions came with her first disappointments. We can trust someone as long as he has not disappointed us. We can be supremely self-confident as long as we believe we are perfect, and so have not disappointed ourselves. But each disappointment corresponds to a question. Why did he do that to me? Why does he react in such a way? Each disappointment Thérèse caused her parents disappointed her, and she was sad about it. Like all of us, Thérèse had this experience. Some people, however, never go beyond the faith of their childhood to enter with hope into a new stage of faith. We can regret this simple innocence as a lost paradise and refuse to look at real-life challenges. But this was not little Carlo's style.

Carlo did not write his memoirs. He experienced his life. He was not over scrupulous and, for that matter, did not like to dwell on his life. So, how do we know if he ever left his childhood's paradise?

ADDIO, NONNO!

The difference between a young child and one who has matured is a series of separations from his mother and father. The cord has to be cut, so to speak, and this is never painless. Psychoanalysts have written reams about it. Everyone goes through these more or less traumatic experiences. And yet, separations must occur if a child is to mature. This is life's learning process. Carlo's first separations were at a very young age, because his parents had professional careers outside the home. Carlo did not yet know how to talk when he was left with young nannies. But these separations, nevertheless, led to joy — the joy of the evening reunion. Carlo would hear the noise of keys in the lock and jump into Daddy's arms when he came through the front door. He was just as much on the lookout for his mother. She knew how to please her little boy, who was fond of good food, by bringing home the little sweets he loved so much.

Other separations lasted longer and were more trying for Carlo. The most difficult would be the death of his maternal grandfather, Antonio Salzano, who had welcomed him to his home in southern Italy. He was the one who saw Carlo take his first steps, and he enjoyed hearing grandson say, "no ... no ... no ... Nonno" — that is, "Grandpa." Carlo was only three years old when his Grandpa died. A few days before this sad event, Carlo, who was baptized at birth, witnessed another sacrament—the Sacrament of the Anointing of the Sick that his Grandpa received during the Last Rites. It was the last sign of the Holy Spirit in his Grandpa's life on earth, the last mark of God's love before he crossed over to the other side. This is a sacrament that continues the closeness that Jesus had with the sick, like Peter's mother-in-law, and even those who had died, like Jairus' daughter, whom he raised from the dead. Jesus touched and healed bodies that were called to share in His Resurrection, after having carried their crosses with Him. It can leave us with a lot of questions. If God loves us, why does He allow suffering? Why does He separate us from the ones we love most? Carlo's family, which was grieving, did not necessarily have the answers to all these questions. What can a little child understand about death when he is only three?

Carlo did not, of course, understand everything, and yet he was not stupid. The young boy, who was knee-high to a grasshopper, saw the great grief his loved ones experienced with the death of Nonno, a great loss he also felt. He saw his mother's tears and her sadness at the loss her father. His Grandma Luana, in particular, was overwhelmed by the loss of the man with whom she had shared her life. She moved to Milan to gain support from her daughter, son-in-law, and grandson. It is not easy to speak to a child about death. We wonder what words his parents and Grandma used to tell him the truth without traumatizing him. But the tears of Carlo's loved ones were enough for him.

Three years is a little too early to have to grow up. Yet, it was an important stage in Carlo's life, his grandma emphasized. Providentially, she found consolation in the joy that her grandson gave her. For her, Carlo embodied the second theological virtue, about which Charles Péguy wrote so well in his poem "A Little Hope." One day, while she was taking care of her little Carlo in Milan, she saw him get agitated and put on his coat. "But where do you want to go like that, my dear?" she asked. "I am going to church, Nonna." "But, we already went on Sunday. What more can we do there?" she asked. "I want us to go pray for Nonno," Carlo replied. "But do you know where Nonno is now?" she asked her grandson. "Yes," Carlo replied. "He went to see Jesus." While grief often shatters our faith, in Carlo it increased the virtue of hope. Nonno was the first of his friends or family to go up to Heaven. The simplicity of his child's heart enabled Carlo to trust in Jesus that, one day, he would be able to see Nonno again. For Carlo, Nonno was not only his Grandpa, but also his brother in the Faith. In the Faith, he had hope he would see him again someday for eternity, in God's presence. That is why he wanted to return to the church to say goodbye to him, as we say farewell. *Addio*, Nonno!

THE FIGHTS IN THE SCHOOLYARD

Carlo's childhood faith merged into the faith of his adolescence. He did not lose his innocence, but he embraced the suffering life brought him.

He would experience his first disappointments mostly in friendship. Friendship is not built in a day. It takes time. It must endure disappointments, skirmishes, and reconciliations. School, incidentally, is where it all takes place for most of us. Many of us have returned from school one day to tell our parents triumphantly that we had just met our best friend. And little by little, we realize that fostering a friendship takes an entire lifetime. Indeed, friendship is built over time. But what can such a little child tell us about time?

In Carlo's schoolyard, there were fights, as there are in every schoolyard in the world. As in society in general, there are inevitably rivalries at school. We all want to be the top student, the most loved, and the most popular, even if sometimes we have to fight to achieve those goals. We can imagine that starting school was a significant step for Carlo, who had previously not had much contact with other children. Given his tender nature, starting school was likely an additional challenge for Carlo. He was not a big shot in the schoolyard. He did not seek to enter school competitions either. He would never be ranked first in his class—either middle school in the Marcelline Tommaseo Institute, which the Sisters of St. Marcellina operate or, later, in high school at the Leo XIII Institute, which the Jesuits run and which is named after a pope. He was an average student, who did his best and knew how to help those who needed him. When his friends had to prepare their notes for the big oral exam of the *terza media*,[14] Carlo helped those who needed to digitize their individual note cards on the computer, even though he had a lot of his own work. Everyone was trying to outdo each other to get the best grade, yet Carlo was not so passionate about his schoolwork. On the other hand, Carlo liked to learn on his own, by reading manuals and opening up other books. Indeed, that is how he discovered his greatest passions: computer science, the saxophone and, of course, learning and living the Faith. Those are the areas in which he excelled. He is known for his skill in computer science (we will talk more about it later), but he became accomplished at playing saxophone, which is a difficult instrument to master. Yet, he learned the saxophone on his own, so well in fact that he could play classical jazz tunes beautifully. Not bad for a self-taught prodigy!

A young female student helped Carlo with his homework after school, because Carlo's mother was often away from home due to her career. The two youngsters got along well. Yet, Carlo's young tutor was a little surprised. Why did a boy with so many abilities not try harder to be the best student in his class? Carlo did not answer. Instead, Carlo worried about those who were in more academic trouble than he was. He helped them with their studies as much as he could.

---

14. The equivalent of a diploma, which includes, in addition, an oral exam in front of the teachers.

In addition, Carlo refused to engage in classroom rivalries. He did not want to participate in academic competitions at school. He was satisfied with doing what his teachers asked him to do, i.e., his homework and to be well-behaved and attentive in class. That was enough for him. In this way, he was happy. One might blame him for not being more ambitious, but, again, Carlo, had other passions. Completing his homework meant spending time with his friends, tinkering at his computer, playing the saxophone, and participating in daily Mass. Everyone has objectives in life, and the young lady who helped Carlo with his nightly homework received a more valuable lesson from her student. She ended up following Carlo to church.

PHOTOCOPYING METHODS

There was another competition Carlo refused to engage in — wearing brand-name clothes. Carlo understood the empty and ephemeral nature of a fashion-crazed culture. Young people at school were becoming enslaved by consumerism. When they saw a bag, sweater, or fashionable shoes, they were ready to do anything to get them. If you look at Carlo's photos, you will see he was dressed like other young people — with jeans, tennis shoes, T-shirts, or shirts. But he did not wear the latest and best clothes, even though he could have, given his parents' wealth. He may have been a little traditional in his apparel, but he was never unfashionable. Sometimes, his friends teased him. They were very proud of being fashionable ... or, at least, of thinking that they were. But how long does fashion last? What good does it do to spend so much money on—literally—the passing fashion? Carlo knew better. He had everything he needed in life. Like Carlo's friends, we can be tempted to have more, buy more, and consume more. But what is the point? We need to learn from Carlo.

Since he did not do what the crowd did, Carlo could seem a little lonely at school. Some students get discouraged and teased by their classmates—the fashion police and other bullies, or because they don't measure up in one type of competition or another. While Carlo was not competitive, his strong faith prevented him from becoming a victim at school, and he also supported his fellow students who were alienated for one reason or another. His friends laughed a little at his piety, but he did not need their approval in that way. Carlo was free. He was an authentic boy who did not try to manipulate others to fit in. Thus, without calling attention to himself, Carlo stood out in what mattered most. All his teachers still remember him today. One of them, from his middle school, said, "Carlo was a budding gentleman." He was a polite and respectful student. But more than that, he cared for others and was always available to offer his help. You either have or do not have class! And Carlo had it, without having to be the coolest one in the middle school. Carlo managed to avoid rivalries with finesse and authenticity.

Like many children of his generation, Carlo was an only child. We have previously said that his parents were not able to have other children during his lifetime, although they would give birth to twins, Michele and Francesca, four years after Carlo's death. Fortunately, Carlo had a paternal cousin named Flavia, with whom he was very close, and who was like his best friend. But at home, he was often alone. So he spent his days reading and learning all about other subjects that interested him. This also left him time to dream and look deep within for the answers to life's most important questions.

Carlo was also often alone when he went to church. But, in reality, he was never alone in his heart. Deep down, Carlo always lived in the presence of God, whom he considered to be his best friend. Worldly competitions and races to success did not interest him. The only race that interested him was the one whose goal was Heaven.

History would prove him right. Carlo's basic attitude would become one of the sentences that characterizes him the best. As he so aptly put it: "We are all born originals, but many of us die as photocopies." In fact, Carlo's originality—his uniqueness—was his holiness. He did not try to be like everyone, no more than he necessarily attempted to be different. He simply endeavored to be himself—his best self. Carlo believed we are all original when we are born, but, with time, we let ourselves be caught up in fashion, influences, and advertisements, and so we all end up looking

alike. Here is a proof that Carlo got it right—Pope Francis
used the expression in the letter that followed the 2018
Synod of Bishops on Young People, Faith and Vocational
Discernment![15] He said he was impressed by Carlo and that
he "very well knew that these mechanisms of communication, advertising, and social networks can be used to make
us sleepy beings, who are dependent on the consumption
and novelties that we can acquire, fanatics of free time, and
prisoners of negativity."

To this end, it has become much more difficult to be
oneself in a world that is saturated by "likes," images, and
the latest craze. For this purpose, Carlo can be a model of
holiness for us. But be warned. Like every model of holiness, this is not about copying and pasting in our lives but,
rather, of seeing Carlo as a model who can inspire us, in
turn, to become our best selves. Pope Francis added:

> Carlo did not fall into a trap. He saw that many
> young people, if they seem to be different, end up, in
> reality, looking like each other, by running behind

---

15. From October 3–28 that year, the world's bishops met at the Vatican,
at Pope Francis' invitation, to discuss the future of the Church with young
people from across the globe. This meeting is called a "synod," from the
ancient Greek "syn" (group) and "odos" (path), i.e., a meeting where the
Church gets back on track together. After the synod, which media worldwide covered, the Holy Father published an "exhortation," in which he
invited young people not to be afraid to take their places in the Church,
and to respond to Christ's call emulating saints like Joan of Arc or new
models like Carlo Acutis.

what powerful people impose on them via mechanisms of consumption and stupor. In this way, they
do not let the gifts that the Lord has made for them
flow into them. They do not offer the world these
personal and unique gifts that the Lord has sown in
each one of them.[16]

Carlo knew how to let his talents flow. These talents
were unique, and he shared them with the world, as we
will see.

ALONE BUT NOT LONESOME

At first, everything seemed easy in Carlo's life.
But let us not rely on appearances. Is it easy
to be comfortable with who you are as a child,
and to resist the pressure of your peers, not to
mention the world at large? Evidently not! Carlo
experienced another difficulty, the difficulty of loneliness.
But Carlo's familial solitude and inner freedom did not drive
him to withdraw into himself. On the contrary, because he
was rooted in Christ, they difficulties turned him toward
others. Through living alone, some people wither away.
They no longer pay attention to how they dress, do not take
care of their bodies, and are no longer interested in those
around them. This would never be the case with Carlo. He
certainly spent a lot of time alone like all children who have

---

16. Post-synodal exhortation *Christus vivit*.

no siblings. But when he was old enough to develop true friendships, he had close friends. This did not protect him from criticism. We can imagine his feelings of loneliness when others laughed at him for not following the crowd when it came to doing this or that nonsense or excluding this or that friend. Or when he went to church by himself, where he was typically the only young person in the midst of many older people.

So, did he withdraw into his little world and live in a bubble to survive? He was certainly tempted to do this, especially since he was, after all, rather privileged. He was lucky to have parents who gave him everything—even the blessing of knowing that he was loved. Given all he had, Carlo could have turned out differently, becoming a spoiled child who lived just for himself and for others. At times, even some Christians can withdraw into their fortress of faith, shielding themselves from the world around them. Carlo worried about such Christians, who only lived in their bubbles. Carlo was human in living his faith. For example, his hair was always disheveled. And yet he was always clean. We did not see him walking around in jeans with holes in them, dirty old T-shirts, or in outdated clothing. He dressed modestly but elegantly. And his free-flowing hair in the wind reflected an inner freedom he demonstrated outwardly. But what distinguished him, above all, was his smile. Carlo smiled at life. For if Carlo lived alone, he was not lonely. He knew all his cousins, class-mates, and even all the people in his building—from the ground floor caretakers to the neighbor on the fifth floor. But how did he do this? It was simple. He smiled at them.

THE SMALL HOPE

Charles Péguy, a writer who died on the battle-fields of the First World War, wrote this line in one of his poems: "God says that what aston-ishes me is hope. And I can't believe it. Hope is a very little insignificant girl."[17] Carlo believed that living as a Christian was not, first of all, nourishing great hopes, but living with a humble hope. Carlo helped us become more hopeful and confident in the future and in eternity. He forbids us from stagnating. Hope is also the patience of accepting that everything is not done yet and needs to be developed and trusting in the Lord that the best is yet to come. This virtue of hope was visible in Carlo's temperament. It started in his early childhood, in the patience he showed while waiting for his parents when their jobs kept them away, and in his friendships that he agreed to form in the long term. It was also evident in the hours he spent in church, without necessarily understanding everything, but with this great hope of finding his best friend there. Carlo was hopeful because God had blessed him with loving, faith-filled parents, whom he obediently

---

17. "Le Porche du Mystère de la deuxième vertu" ("The Portico of the Mystery of the Second Virtue"), by Charles Péguy.

trusted. But Carlo was also the hope of his parents, who were inspired by his childlike faith, a faith that enabled them to love God and their son all the more.

THE WORD OF GOD

Then his mother and his brethren came to him, but they could not reach him for the crowd. And he was told, "Your mother and your brethren are standing outside, desiring to see you." But he said to them, "My mother and my brethren are those who hear the word of God and do it." One day he got into a boat with his disciples, and he said to them, "Let us go across to the other side of the lake. So they set out." (Luke 8:19–22)

LIFE QUESTIONS

➤ How do I respond to the sadness in my life? What makes me the saddest, and what consoles me?

➤ Do I love the family God has given me, with both their strengths and weaknesses? Do I appreciate the time I get to share with my loved ones?

➤ Do I leave room for relaxing and leisure in my life? Do I endlessly ask what we will be doing later? Do I know how to live in the present moment?

➤ What are my biggest dreams? Do my hopes bring me closer to the hope of happiness and Heaven Jesus gives us, or do they lead me away from it?

➤ What is my hope?

PRAYER TO GOD

O God, my hope, I put all my hopes in You. You know all of my dreams, ambitions, and plans. You also know my doubts, uncertainties, loneliness, and disappointments. Help me to rediscover the great hope of my childhood, this expectation that only You can fulfill—that of knowing and meeting You. Show me Your presence in my life—this divine face that You reveal through Jesus Christ. Teach me to rediscover Christ in each of the brothers and sisters that You have given me. And lead me home to Heaven, and help me lead others.

Chapter 3
Friend of Jesus

THE WAY TO HEAVEN

When we retrace our lives, we like to see various stages and dramatic changes in our favor. We fear a life that is insipid and boring, because it would be too ordinary and one-dimensional. We think that to live passionately we have to experience intense ups-and-downs ... but not too many downs. We aim for the top. But we take detours, because the path that goes straight up frightens us. Yet, sometimes living intensely is the only thing we seek. We never want to yawn or say something trite, like a hero from a Jack Kerouac novel. Like a candle in the night, we want to burn, burn, and burn. But we're afraid we'll burn out. The challenge is to find zest in our routine and the extraordinary in our ordinary lives. Carlo lived this way. For example, he was present to others in the subway, where everyone is glum, with a greeting and smile. In the midst of the dreariness of daily life, while everyone is dreaming of vacation, trips, and adventures, Carlo experienced this adventure of holiness, here and now. Nothing less! Here was a life project and an ambition! It was an adventure was full of colors and surprises.... This was Carlo's life.

But what were the stages of Carlo's life adventure? When did he change his life? When did he really start to seek holiness? There was no breakdown on his spiritual journey, no shocking story, no point of no return except for the fatal illness that ended his earthly journey. Carlo did not have an apparition of Jesus, the Blessed Virgin Mary, angels, or Heaven and all it contains. There was no "before or after" for Carlo. His child's faith gradually grew into an adolescent's faith. Very often, we think that conversion is a denial, a rejection of what we have been or a forgetting of our past. A classic example is a person who converts on his deathbed or asks for Baptism *in extremis*, therefore rejecting all the bad habits of his past life. However, it is precisely his whole life, with its joys and disappointments, that has led him up to the dramatic turn. God writes straight with crooked lines, as the saying goes. Yes, God writes straight, though we have the impression He makes us zigzag. We sometimes take detours and prefer to forget them. We would like to start everything over, as if we could erase all our bad choices. We take satisfaction in thinking that we have turned the page and things will not be the same as before. We might even think we can change our lives the same way we change our T-shirts. But is that really holiness? Carlo's growth in holiness was not without its challenges. In addition, while each one of our personal, familial, and national stories has moments we would rather hide, Carlo is the first prospective saint whose history we have on the computer he left behind. He was not inclined to hide anything from us. Carlo's history consists of hours and hours of research. These include questions that he asked himself or that others asked him, and to which he insatiably looked for answers. There are also photos of churches he dreamed of visiting and images of miracles about which he had heard. He died too early to gain answers to all of his questions. He also often made mistakes or only had one imperfect answer to a research question. But he never stopped wanting to find an answer, especially the ones that him helped navigate the highway to Heaven.

But sometimes we prefer more winding paths. We like to hear about the conversion stories of gangsters who dramatically changed their lives through God's mercy, and to see films about wicked people whose lives are ultimately redeemed. Consequently, we can have a hard time appreciating ordinary holiness. Yet, if there is a place in Heaven for criminals and prostitutes, there is a place for ordinary holiness as well. Our lives are also imperfect, but we are not all former addicts or converted big shots. Nevertheless, is our conversion any less valuable? To draw a parallel, we often talk about the parable of the prodigal son and the merciful father. But there is another brother, who is too often forgotten. He may be more like us — the one who did not roll in the mud with the pigs or squander his father's heritage. He is a brother who stayed in business and was so ordinarily holy that we forget that he was also invited to the festive banquet. So, we often, like the second son, stay outside to watch these prodigal sons return with extraordinary testimonies. Instead of experiencing joy, thanks to others, we forget to celebrate. We tell ourselves that this "simple" Catholicism that we inherited is boring compared to these great stories of spectacular conversions. Carlo's life teaches us to value ordinary holiness. His life is a straighter line, a pathway to Heaven he invites us to take.

VIA VIATORES QUAERIT

It is impressive to count all the trips Carlo took in his short life. Yet, his family vacations were not to the grandest tourist destinations. Of course, he spent a lot of time at his grandparents' home on the magnificent Mediterranean coast. But he also took bigger trips with his parents, and he chose the destinations. He did not ask his parents to take him to Monte Carlo or Cancún. If he traveled far away, it was because he was looking for someone: *Via viatores quaerit*: "I am the path that always welcomes travelers." These are the words that St. Augustine heard in his prayers. Augustine himself traveled a lot in the twilight of the ancient Roman

Empire—from North Africa to Rome, and as far as Milan. There, when he was the farthest away from home, he met St. Ambrose, who formed him in the Faith and baptized him. Centuries later, Carlo was the traveler who found his path. He was lucky to make a dream journey to northern Greece, in the region of the Meteora, which contains Christian monasteries that are perched on top of cliffs and rocky gray peaks carved by erosion. There, he encountered the Orthodox Christian world, including hieromonks.[18] When he saw believers approach the iconostasis[19] and kiss its icons, he was touched by the devotion of their faith. It is amazing to think that St. Paul established some of the first Christian communities in Greece, far away from the Holy Land; and, today, we can still walk in his footsteps.

Each of his pilgrimages helped Carlo grow in his faith. In February 2005, he made his first pilgrimage to Lourdes. In 2006, he went to Fatima, the little village in Portugal, where the Blessed Mother appeared to three children in 1917. Carlo became aware of many things during this pilgrimage. The devotion of the little shepherds of Fatima especially touched him. They were like him in that they were neither

---

18. In the Orthodox Church, a hieromonk is a monk who has been ordained as a priest.
19. The iconostasis is a partition in Byzantine rite churches that serves as a dividing point between the nave and the sanctuary and, symbolically, as an intersection between time and eternity. Icons, which are often made out of wood or stone, are placed on this partition. They are venerated by the faithful, not as such, but for what they represent.

important nor desirous to make a name for themselves. They simply wanted to know God and love Him with all their hearts. Francisco, Jacinta, and Lucia were the three children tending their sheep when the Blessed Mother appeared to them. In reading the story of the messages the Virgin Mary gave these shepherd children, Carlo grew more aware that Hell really existed. He also understood more deeply the Passion Jesus suffered and which Mary witnessed at the foot of the Cross. The message that Mary gave the children of Fatima did not add anything to the gospel, but rather provided a renewed call to conversion. Our Lady of Fatima sadly said: "Pray, pray very much, and make sacrifices for sinners, for many souls go to Hell because there is no one to sacrifice and pray for them."[20] In 1917, when the apparitions took place in Portugal, and the sun miraculously danced in the sky before thousands of pilgrims who had come to pray with the children, the world urgently needed conversion. The First World War was still going on, the

---

20. Excerpted from Mary's fourth apparition in Fatima on August 19, 1917. Lucia de Jesus Rosa dos Santos was born on March 22, 1907 in Fatima. Thus, she was ten during the apparitions. Her cousin Francisco Marto was nine. And Jacinta, Francisco's sister, was only seven. They tended their sheep in a place known as the Cova da Iria. The messages of Fatima, which were an exhortation to prayer and conversion, would guide the Church through a century of persecution and reverberate to such an extent that, today, we find statues of Our Lady of Fatima in churches around the world. After a failed attempt on his life May 13, 1981, Pope John Paul II came to the Portuguese shrine to give thanks, placing the bullet that brushed against his heart in the crown that decorates the Virgin Mary's statue.

Communist Revolution convulsed Russia only weeks later, and the world ignored Pope Benedict XV's pleas for peace. What could the little children of Fatima do in the face of so much upheaval? They did not apparently do anything great in their lifetimes. But today, Fatima has become a great shrine and has inspired a renewal of faith in Portugal and the world.

These little children influenced the world much more than they thought. While they were alive, they made small sacrifices, which were offered for world peace and the conversion of sinners. Yet, what can little shepherds in rural Portugal sacrifice? For that matter, without a lot of wealth and power, what can we ourselves offer? We can offer ourselves! We can sacrifice our own will and pride. This may not seem like much. But it can help change the world when united with Jesus, who offered Himself for the whole world in His Passion. We too can learn to offer ourselves. We can discipline our passions by gaining strength from Christ's Passion. This can start off as a simple physical reality, a child's sacrifice. For example, we can start with a small sacrifice of fasting—a little renunciation of the belly's pleasure. These small sacrifices can be like the offering of the widow in the gospels who did not have much to give, but who put her last coins in the poor box. Her offering was worth more than the multimillionaire's millions or the surplus of those who were well off, because she gave everything she had. To offer something is to give from one's heart and life.

And the spirit of sacrifice is to offer oneself. Carlo, who was terribly gluttonous, embraced this spirit of renunciation. He learned to give of himself, little by little. He abstained from little sweet treats or deprived himself of his favorite films. These sacrifices were not great feats or masterpieces, like a Monet, but they were sincere and enthusiastic. Carlo's world had different problems than the world of 1917. But his world still needed prophets and witnesses—men and women of faith. Carlo experienced no special apparitions. He was not any greater or more influential than the Fatima shepherds. Unbridled consumerism, Islamic terrorism, and institutionalized debauchery were all very frightening to him—almost as much as Hell scared the little Fatima shepherds. What could he do about these world problems? Carlo could not save the world. He knew that was Jesus' job. But he developed a spiritual friendship with these shepherd children from the previous century. And so he decided to live like them—with a spirit of sacrifice in which he made his whole life a gift to God and others. He grew in devotion during his pilgrimage to Fatima. Among all the treasures he brought back from Fatima, he learned how to pray the Rosary[21] and discover the greatness of his friendship with

---

21. The Rosary is a prayer tool many have heard of. A rosary has five sets of ten beads that are linked together. They correspond to ten Hail Marys for each mystery, and five Our Fathers, which begins each mystery. A crucifix links all of the beads. Depending on the day of the week, Catholics are invited to meditate on the Joyous, Sorrowful, Luminous, or Glorious Mysteries, which correspond to important events in the lives of Jesus and

Christ. He followed the life of Jesus with Mary. In the most joyful, sorrowful, luminous, and glorious moments of Jesus' time on earth, Carlo learned more deeply how Jesus gave His life for him. He prayed these mysteries in the spiritual bouquet called the "crown of roses," the Rosary. When we are young, it can seem difficult to keep concentrating on this seemingly monotonous prayer. With the simplicity of a child, the Rosary repeats words and scenes and offers them to God as a gift. But the Rosary is there to grab us and keep us from being distracted. It helps us learn to talk to God. It repeats the words that He Himself taught us in the Gospel. Carlo learned to pray the Rosary well, not to repeat it mechanically and as rapidly as a machine gun. He knew its purpose was an intimate encounter with God. God became Carlo's best friend, because Carlo spent daily time talking to and listening to Him.

JESUS AMIGO

For Carlo, Jesus' Heart was the symbol of His whole life and His love. It is this love the He freely gave for us. The most beautiful eucharistic gesture was, to Carlo, to put his head on Jesus' Heart, like St. John did during the Last Supper. This act means receiving Jesus in your heart at

---

Mary, e.g., the Nativity (Jesus' birth), the Wedding Feast at Cana, and Christ's Crucifixion and Resurrection.

Holy Communion, so that His Heart can speak intimately to yours. Carlo's familiarity with Jesus was matched only by his love for Him. The prayers that he wrote, and even his way of speaking to Jesus, showed that they lived together in a true intimacy, an intimacy to which he also invited his relatives and friends. Carlo knew that faith was not simply belief, but a very personal friendship with God. At the same time, it was not just something he could experience by himself. Carlo had a very traditional faith, which always remained alive for him.

He often spoke of the "Heart of Jesus." In France, when we speak of the "Sacred Heart," we think, above all, of the immense church in Montmartre, which was built in 1923, only a century ago. When Carlo spoke about the Sacred Heart, he noted how Christ's Heart was pierced on the Cross for us. He was very impressed by the meditations of the French nun, St. Margaret Mary Alacoque, who had incredible visions of Jesus in her convent in Paray-le-Monial. She saw Jesus' open Heart, "this heart that so loved the world," as she would say in 1675. However, so often "this heart has received only indifference in exchange for all His love," Margaret Mary lamented. In the nineteenth century, amid the Industrial Revolution, the devotion to the Sacred Heart took off. Man had invented the machine. Everything was mechanized. Everything was mass produced, and man only a link in this entire operation. God Himself was no longer necessary, some men thought, because science and "progress" had the answer for everything. God and man were no longer sacred. To respond to this misguided societal movement, the Church proclaimed the Sacred Heart of Jesus, reminding the world that God is not dead. The Sacred Heart of Jesus still beats in the midst of the world and for the world. In the Battle of Sedan in 1870, the first death machines and military machine guns mowed down hundreds of French soldiers on the front line in only a few hours. However, all of France providentially responded to this terrible loss, coming together to build the Sacred Heart Basilica of Montmartre above Paris, to help Jesus shower the love of His Sacred Heart on the world. Many missionaries—men as well as women—would establish religious communities devoted to the Sacred Heart to proclaim Christ's love to and for the world, which people too often forget.

More than a century later, Carlo saw a need for the Sacred Heart's love, a need for God's compassion and mercy towards today's man. If the Sacred Heart of Jesus could save the world from machines and modernity, the digital age needs to be saved from a system where everything is calculated and digitized. God's love is not calculated. He is madly and passionately in love with this world, which urgently needs to rediscover compassion. Carlo was surprised to see so many horrible things on the television news and so much indifference in the world—as if we no longer had time in a world that was too busy to notice suffering. Perhaps our daily schedules are too full, like the 24/7 programs on our TV channels. After the big newscast, the forecast, the advertising, and the bad shows and films, everyone goes to bed. We can get into bad routines.

Carlo did not want to be a Christian who was programmed. He wanted to live and love with a heart that was open to the world, while being inspired by the Holy Spirit. This sometimes surprised his parents. Thus, he often brought friends over without much warning. One day, when he saw two brothers fighting in school, he invited them home after school. Carlo did not do this to lecture them, but simply to help them play and make up. For Carlo, loving the Sacred Heart of Jesus was to make His Passion our passion. Every first Friday of the month, Carlo would emotionally recall Christ's Passion, when Jesus gave us the greatest proof of His love. It was not about doing something more. Carlo was already doing a lot. He participated in daily Mass and fasted when the Church asked for it, especially during Lent. He did not smoke or drink alcohol, except for a little glass of champagne so as not to be bad company on Christmas Eve. The first Friday of the month was not about adding a sacrifice, but simply recalling Christ's Passion and being more present to Him on that specific day, as if he were at the foot of the Cross with Jesus, and especially at the Hour of Mercy—3 p.m.—when Jesus died for us on the Cross. He found his model of love and friendship in the open Heart of Jesus.

THE FRIEND WHO HAS FORGIVEN EVERYTHING

The most faithful friend is the one who knows how to both forgive and ask for forgiveness. By becoming aware, as he grew up, of the love God had for him, Carlo discovered the serious-ness of taking God for granted. He wanted to live in God's mercy so he could be united to His Love as much as possible. He knew that God wants to forgive us, and yet He gives us freedom to love and reconcile ourselves with Him. If we think that Carlo is holy because he never did anything bad, all we have to know is how often he went back to church to ask God's forgiveness. All great saints have been humble enough to recognize their sins and reflect on David's Psalm, which expresses the cry of a sinner who calls out for God's mercy:

> Have mercy on me, O God, according to thy steadfast love; according to thy abundant mercy blot out my transgressions. Wash me thoroughly from my iniq-uity, and cleanse me from my sin! For I know my transgressions, and my sin is ever before me. Against thee, thee only, have I sinned, and done that which is evil in thy sight, so that thou art justified in thy sentence and blameless in thy judgment. (Ps. 51:1–4)

St. Augustine wrote his *Confessions*. Carlo did not leave us anything similar. But we have his confessor's testimony.

While remaining faithful to the seal of Confession, Don
Mario Perego, his parish priest, discreetly bore witness to
Carlo's great desire to grow in holiness:

> Carlo was a young man who was exceptionally trans-
> parent. He really wanted to progress in loving his
> parents, God, his classmates, and those who loved
> him less. He wanted to apply himself in his studies
> to educate himself in his catechism class as well as
> in school and computer science.

Confession is the secret story of the love between Carlo
and God. The point is not about trying to know what
Carlo might have said in his confessions. What counts is
to understand how this process of asking God for forgiveness in Confession made him grow in his love. We can
be certain that Carlo went to Confession just before his
First Communion in June 1998. He was only seven years
old. All children who prepare their First Communion
often experience, on this occasion, their first Sacrament
of Reconciliation. When we are seven or eight, what can
we do that is serious? Not much, perhaps. But his parents
taught him to apologize when he made big mistakes, even
when they were done accidentally. He believed, therefore, that it was normal to ask God for forgiveness. To get
ready to receive Jesus in the Eucharist, Carlo would go to
weekly Confession. He explained that "asking for forgiveness and being reconciled with God is like rekindling the

fire of your hot-air balloon and discarding the stones that are weighing your basket down." Carlo thought that even his smallest sins were like cords that reattached to the ground and prevented him from taking off. In his life, he wanted to figure out how to free himself from them. Yet, awareness of his sins led Carlo to be humble, not discouraged. He liked to repeat the centurion's words: "Lord, I am not worthy to have you come under my roof" (Matt. 8:8). Carlo's spiritual sensitivity struck his confessor so much that he still thinks about Carlo's example when he has to discern complex pastoral situations in exercising his priestly duties. Carlo had a sensitive soul and so learned how to discern well.

MY BUDDY CARLO

Carlo's friends were jealous of his friendship with Jesus. When he went to church, he looked happy and seemed to know what was going on. He appeared to know Jesus and what the Sacrifice of the Mass meant. More than anything, Carlo called God his friend. In the midst of where he lived, everyone seemed to have dozens of friends in common, but many were missing the most important one. Carlo wanted his friends to have this friend in common—Jesus, the one who made friends with everyone. By becoming Carlo's friend, other young people were drawn to becoming God's friend as well.

Carlo wanted to be a friend to others the way that Jesus was a friend to him. He did not try to add to his list of contacts, become the most popular person in his middle school, gain more followers online, or send the most retweets. He simply wanted to be a friend. He had such a friendship with his cousin Flavia. Carlo's parents have kept the board games that Carlo and Flavia liked to play together—from chess to Monopoly. We can imagine the long games that drew them even closer together as cousins. Carlo talked at length about what friendship meant to him. He conceived of it as unselfish concern for others. Friendship is not about finding people who make us feel good, but about accepting the people life has put on our path and loving them where they're at, though seeking to draw them closer to God. In Italian, to tell someone you like him, you say: *"Ti voglio bene,"* which is to say, "I wish you well." That is how Carlo conceived of friendship. He did not find friends by getting himself noticed. He did not attract them with money or popularity, although he could have. What drew so many people to Carlo was his ability to make people laugh and smile.

He did not try to be the class clown or the braggart at the back of the class. But Carlo knew how to make people laugh and thereby share his joyful smile. Carlo invited friends home with him to lift their spirits, especially when they were alone or going through difficult times. Andrea and Francesco, two brothers whose parents were in the middle of separating, recalled an afternoon they spent with Carlo. Whereas everyone else was embarrassed about their family situation but did not dare address it with them, Carlo became their loyal friend. He invited them home, so they could play together and think about something else. He knew that others' homes were not necessarily as joyful as his.

Carlo also sought to befriend the shyest kids in his class, and he did not like it when children were excluded from activities. Carlo was clearly not the strongest one in his class, nor the most intellectually gifted, nor the best soccer player. He was not even the most gifted one among his friends, except in computer science. But when he saw kids excluded, mocked, or harassed, Carlo stepped forward. Perhaps this was because his best friend was unjustly perse-cuted, excluded, mistreated, and ultimately crucified. He did not want to see any child treated in a similar way. So, when one of his friends got harassed in the schoolyard, Carlo intervened decisively, yet nonviolently: by taking the hand of the child being excluded or ridiculed and walking away together. They would leave the angry instigators alone with each other.

Ambra M. was one of Carlo's friends. She was also born in 1991. She shared his passion for music. Today, she has achieved her dream of opening an upscale fresh-fish restau-rant in one of Milan's most popular neighborhoods. This magnificent woman lovingly and emotionally remembers

Carlo, saying she still speaks to him in her prayers: "With Carlo, I have a friend in Heaven who watches over me. Each time I have a problem, I know that I can talk to him about it. I am not as holy as Carlo was, but the fact of having known him is already lifting me up."

Federico O. was also one of Carlo's old friends. They studied together at the middle school of the Marcelline Tommaseo Institute. Today, he is a graduate of the Polytechnic University of Milan. He is an engineer, which would have been Carlo's dream if he had lived long enough. But Federico is not nostalgic or regretful. Today, he rejoices that Carlo's joyful testimony is going beyond Italy's borders. He recalls his infectious joy and his gift for computer-science. He often thinks about him.

He did this recently again, more specifically on the occasion of the death of Steve Jobs, the founder of Apple. Federico remembers that Carlo really admired Jobs, who, in some ways, was a model for him because of his innovative talent, entrepreneurial daring, and perseverance. Carlo, who was passionate about technology and computer science, was a big fan of Macintosh and other Apple products. To receive a Mac, Carlo had to give up two years of Christmas and birthday gifts! And to this day, Federico uses a Mac on Carlo's advice, although he is much more grateful for something else Carlo gave him. Carlo taught Federico to pray, a gift for which he will be forever grateful.

HAVING FUN WITHOUT LOSING CONTROL

An anecdote from Carlo's life can teach us a lesson. At the beginning of this century, there were no computer tablets. But there were all sorts of video game consoles. Carlo had a whole range of games in his home, such as car-racing and action-adventure games. He enjoyed them a lot. There were no longer any secrets for him in Super Mario, Pokémon, and Zelda. Carlo's interest in computers games also posed a challenge for his parents, because this type of entertainment did not exist in their childhood. With the arrival of the game console, they found themselves confronted with a new problem at home — the power of screens and the addiction they could generate. In addition, they were a little overwhelmed by the technical aspects. Carlo's father admitted that he did not even know how to turn the console on and that he needed Carlo's help to operate the games.

Yet, while they did not understand the technical aspects of these game, Carlo's parents became rather quickly aware of their risks. They knew Carlo really enjoyed playing with his console. But they quickly imposed the rule that no more than two hours a week would be dedicated to video games. Was this too much or not enough? It didn't matter. It was the rule. Evidently, it's not easy for children to resist these games. Carlo often wanted to play. There's a reason why

Sega's French ads once proclaimed, "Sega is stronger than you!" Video games are very addictive. Carlo's mother sometimes had to raise her voice. Like all good things, video games should be moderately used. Carlo gradually embraced his parents' rule, which helped him to distinguish between the virtual world and real life.

If Carlo succeeded in limiting his video-game consumption, he realized that his friends also struggled with the addictive nature of video games. One day, he invited several friends to his home. At first, everyone was having fun. But after a while, his friends were completely engrossed, and then some got angry when they lost. Others became unbearable because they boasted about their triumph. Then, they all started shouting and crying when their parents asked them to come home. Video games controlled his friends. That day, Carlo, who had been alerted to distance himself from the virtual world, was genuinely surprised by how the afternoon had turned out. He was disappointed because he expected to have a good time with friends. In the end, he saw the day conclude with scenes of tears and tantrums. Thanks to this episode, he realized that screens could be completely alienating. He would recall this when he got older and discovered that he had a real talent for everything that is digital, which went hand in hand with his fascination for tools. This would truly help him keep his real-life priorities in mind. His example shows us that temperance is also involved in our recreational activities.

TAMING HIS GLUTTONY

Carlo knew he wasn't perfect, which included his struggles to eat in moderation. It was a flaw he inherited from his mother. She laughs a lot about it today. He was a *magnaccione*, as the Romans say—a big glutton. His puffy cheeks gave it away. Nutella was his weakness. Yet, Carlo would not indulge his flaw. While growing up, he would become very slender, which was not easy. When home alone, Carlo was tempted to eat all sorts of things in his parents' pantry. St. Augustine stole pears. He related this episode in his *Confessions*. He did not, incidentally, steal out of greed, but for the pleasure of violating a taboo. Carlo took jars of Nutella and, in his case, it was to consume their contents. Every century has its relatively minor sins. It was the theft of these pears that would awaken little Augustine's conscience. Carlo would experience something similar with Nutella, gradually realizing his little sins of theft and gluttony could negatively impact other matters. These included the trust his parents gave him or a certain bondage to food, which could interfere with his other relationships. A little sacrifice corresponds to a little sin. When he was only a small child, Carlo resolved, especially during Lent, to deprive himself of Nutella. Those who are gluttons understand the struggle. When our resolve is weak, we must be strong in our resolutions. We tell ourselves we must not abuse good things. Then, we finally decide to deprive ourselves of it. This might seem easy at first. But we can end up thinking about it all day long. Our stomach growls, even though we have just eaten. We tell ourselves that, in the end, a little spoonful will not hurt anyone and, wham, we become tempted and lose the entire benefit of this small sacrifice. It took time for Carlo to become more temperate. Mrs. Acutis became aware of Carlo's progress, which added to the astonishment she had for her son.

NATURE'S FRIEND

Carlo's love of animals was also surprising. In this way, he reminds us a little of St. Francis who, according to the *fioretti*,[22] sang "Brother Sun and Sister Moon," and talked with birds and wolves. Carlo also was sensitive to creation and all life, even the smallest life. This ranged from a struggling ladybug, which he would sensitively pull out of the local municipal pool, to the puzzlement of the lifeguards on duty, to the defense of other animals he would encounter. It was important for Carlo to respect the environment, including the habitats of the animal world. When he walked in the forest with his parents, Carlo would fill his pockets with all

---

22. St. Francis' life was told by one of his friends, Br. Rufino, who lived with him and collected a number of anecdotes. All these stories are called *fioretti*—"little flowers" because they are like roses in God's garden. Even if they are sometimes embellished, they always speak well of some virtue of the great saint's holiness. These include Francis' humility, poverty, and simplicity of heart and soul.

the papers and cigarette butts he found lying around. His father insisted on buying Carlo a device to pick up trash, a pole so his son could avoid getting his hands dirty on these family excursions. Another time, while at the beach, Carlo put on his mask and fins and used his inflatable boat to remove all the garbage he found on the ocean floor near the seashore.

During the summer of 2004, while he was on vacation at his grandparents' home near Naples with one of his cousins, Carlo blew his top. While walking, he met some young people his age who were "having fun" stomping on lizards and finishing off the reptiles with a rock. While to some these actions might seem harmless, Carlo knew we should not wantonly destroy living things. Carlo became so angry that he cried. His parents consoled him, saying "It's okay. It's not that serious!" Yet, as he got older, Carlo would become even more sensitive to the protection of life, including when he learned about bioethical issues regarding human life. We will see this later.

Carlo had two little cats, four dogs, and some red fish at home. Each time he saw an abandoned animal, he asked his parents to adopt it. As he was gifted in creating short films, Carlo had fun making his pets the heroes of his videos, similar to the *Life of Pi* and the Chronicles of Narnia. But making dogs and cats act in a film was not always easy. He had to be very patient. Nonetheless, with a little perseverance, Carlo managed to put together a whole series of videos. One evening, he invited all his neighbors to come look at his first short film. It was called *Stellina, La Cicciona* (Stellina, the Fat Lady). It was the story of one of his cats who did not leave his home. Another episode followed the adventures of his dog, a magnificent Doberman named Briciola, who, in real life, scared everyone on the street. Actually, he was the nicest animal in the world and the pet Carlo liked most. His playful nickname for Briciola was the "dog with seven demons." Finally, there was his mother's dog, Chiara, whom he ironically named, not the "king of the canines," but the "king of the rats." Chiara terrorized all of the neighborhood dogs. *Cave canem!* "Beware of the dog!" This dog did not let anyone violate her turf. She barked at any would-be intruder, protecting everything that belonged to her mistress, as if she were the guardian of an impregnable fortress. You were not to bother her.

In short, Carlo was surrounded by quite a menagerie. With his small kennel, life did not lack tribulations. In addition, his short films gained notice. Carlo had the gift of making everyone laugh. His funniest video was undoubtedly the one where Chiara, the terrible dog, became the neighborhood's empress and made life hard for the family's cats, who rebelled against her. Chiara played the game so well that you'd think she went to acting school! Meanwhile, Little Cleo, the male cat in the household, was really cunning. He conspired to conquer the world of dogs and dominate the whole earth. That led Poldo, another dog, to intervene as the minister of foreign affairs, trying to restore calm to the kingdom. However, Briciola let Poldo down and joined the cats' revolt. In short, all of Carlo's videos were creative, and everyone had a good time laughing.

His video editing remained rather basic, and his short films didn't become Hollywood blockbusters, but Carlo was a budding director. In the face of his brief life, we can only wonder if he would have become a great filmmaker! But that doesn't matter. The main thing for Carlo was not to dream about his life, but to live out his dreams. Rather than stay glued to his screen and watch life go by from the sofa, he literally became the "actor" of his life and created his own happiness. It didn't take much for him to have fun. All the resources that he needed were in his imagination.

Yet, Carlo had a dream that he held in common with many of the world's children. Carlo dreamed to see dolphins. Films such as *Free Willy* and *Flipper* captivated his generation. But Carlo didn't just want to see dolphins on the big screen or in a little pool at a nearby water park. Carlo, who loved his liberty, desired to see dolphins frolicking free in the ocean! While some kids pray to pass their tests or discern their vocation, Carlo prayed to see dolphins. But does God worry about a child's trivial prayer? Doesn't He have more urgent petitions to answer than this kind of "whim"? We can ask ourselves this question. Yet, how can we say one prayer is more legitimate than another? What deserves to be asked of God? We need to rediscover the simplicity of a child's heart, so we can believe anew that God loves to answer our prayers—even the most insignificant ones. We must rediscover perseverance in prayer toward the one who, from all eternity, has only desired one thing—to love us: "Ask, and it will be given you" (Matt. 7:7). God is not afraid to be bothered. He who is omniscient knows every one of our requests. And when it is just and well-intentioned, and so conforms with His will, He is pleased to grant it.

We can clearly see this in Jesus' life. Whether He was at table and the adulterous woman threw herself at his feet to ask for His forgiveness, or when little Zacchaeus climbed up a sycamore to see His Savior, Jesus responded to their requests. No pain or joy is so insignificant that it doesn't interest God. He is not indifferent to any of our problems or dreams. He listens to each prayer that comes from a sincere heart. And it is with this crazy hope that Carlo said this prayer: "Mom, I asked Jesus for this big gift." His mother worried. Where was her son going to lead her now? "I asked Jesus if I could see some dolphins." His mother restrained herself from laughing. But she knew her son, and so she knew he was serious. If he prayed this prayer, it was authentic. And God granted it in the summer of 2004, during an outing off the coast of Santa Margherita Ligure, where his family owned a little boat. It is one of the

most idyllic Italian coasts, with its turquoise waters and old
monastery near the famous Cinque Terre.[23] It was there that
Carlo's dream came true, a time shared with his paternal
grandfather so wonderful that Carlo Acutis Sr., became
emotional in recalling it:

> When I think of the happiest times I spent with
> Carlo, it is this day that I think about. We were
> out at sea, hoping to see some dolphins. But we
> hardly saw any. Most often, we only saw the wings
> of distant birds, which blended into the hollows of
> the sea. But suddenly, we found ourselves near an
> entire family of dolphins. Dozens of them were flying
> around the boat. This lasted almost a half hour. I
> couldn't believe it. I had never seen anything like
> it. It was like a dream, an unforgettable moment.
> All of us in the boat felt so much joy and happiness
> before this sight.

That day, our Carlo didn't forget his small camera. When
we look at the film he took, we can see he was so excited
by the event that he took photos from every angle. The
dolphins appeared from everywhere—from the port side
and the starboard side. Carlo's overflowing joy was irrepress-
ible. This treasured memory lives on for his grandfather.

---

23. A group of centuries-old villages on the Italian Riviera coastline.

THE VIRTUE OF TEMPERANCE

We sometimes wonder what role pleasure plays in the life of a Christian. After all, God enjoys loving us. There is a little church named San Giovanni all'Oglio in a remote place that Carlo visited in Rome, along the city's ramparts. Above the door's lintel, we can read "For God's pleasure." This sheds light on the true meaning of indulgences. To indulge in something means taking pleasure in doing something.[24] God enjoys giving us signs of His love. We can also enjoy loving as He loves us. But sometimes, our pleasures are disordered by sin. Temperance is the virtue that teaches us to moderate our attraction to pleasures and find a balance when using everything God gives us. Jean de La Fontaine speaks of this virtue in his fable "The Dog Who Carries His Master's Dinner Round His Neck," saying "Temperance should be learned by dogs, and

---

24. Indulgences are often misunderstood. They have continued to be a real sign of division among Christians. While they were to be a sign of God's love for men, they have often become the sign of a scandal. They have been misunderstood as "simony" or the selling of sacraments for money, which has been an issue since the Acts of the Apostles. Simony takes its name from Simon Magus, who pretended he was a real Christian whereas he sold prayers. But Carlo knew that an indulgence was not that at all. They are gifts from God from the treasure house of the Church. Each time he went on a pilgrimage, he tried to seek God's indulgences in an authentic process of faith, as it is written in the entrance of Roman churches: "*indulgentia plenaria quotidiana ac perpetua*," which can be translated as: "Here, God gives the world a sign of His love by completely forgiving all sins every day and forever."

men remain unteachable as dogs!" So, what can temperance teach us? Too often, temperance is perceived as something that eradicates enjoyment, and thus Christian education and formation as promising lukewarm fulfillment at best. This is false! Temperance doesn't entail this, for as God told the lukewarm Laodiceans, "I will spew you out of my mouth" (Rev. 3:16). Carlo provides us with a good example. Our young friend was on fire with God's love! His temperance moderated his passions to give freer rein to his unique passion, which was his passion for the love of others and the love of God.

Carlo knew how to love passionately yet reasonably, without being excessive or extreme. Today, we can no longer love animals without being a vegan. We no longer think a boy or girl can simply be friends without imagining they are hiding something from us. When we are not in a relationship and try to be chaste, people wonder if we are sick or just strange. The problem with many people is that they have allowed their passions to go mad. Reason helps moderate passions, calming their excesses and reviving their lukewarmness. Carlo knew how to love animals and protect them, without idolizing them. He knew how to love his friends without having to possess them physically. He also knew how to be alone, to take time to know God better and thereby know himself better. Carlo lived the virtue of temperance, a virtue that is no longer fashionable, but one that we young people, and even older people, need.

Carlo's temperance was the exact opposite of insensitivity — insensitivity to love, the world, our neighbor, and God. Carlo had a heart that was authentically sensitive to the world around him. He did not suppress his passions but discovered the pleasure we experience in doing good. It was the pleasure of a beautiful hike in the mountains, an evening with friends, a pilgrimage to Fatima, a nice family meal, or some good ice cream on the streets of Rome. It was the pleasure of giving joy to those who did not have it or spending time alone with God. Carlo personified the virtue of temperance.

THE WORD OF GOD

[Jesus] said to him the third time, "Simon, son of John, do you love me?" Peter was grieved because he said to him the third time, "Do you love me?" And he said to him, "Lord, you know everything; you know that I love you." (John 21:17)

LIFE QUESTIONS

➢ Who is my best friend? What is the best that I wish for my friends?

➢ Am I aware of what a blessing it is to have friends? Am I attentive to those who do not have any friends?

➤ When was the last time I asked forgiveness from my parents or friends? Do I manage to ask God for forgiveness and forgive myself?

➤ What angers me the most in life? Am I aware that I can let myself be carried away by my passions? What do I do — or can I do — to fight against them?

➤ When do I enjoy doing good?

PRAYER TO GOD

Sacred Heart of Jesus, have mercy on me. Sacred Heart of Jesus, I trust you. Sacred Heart of Jesus who shed your blood for me, teach me to love like You.

Chapter 4
The Miracle of Love

THE CUP THAT SHINES AND THE CROWN THAT DOES NOT FADE

The Champs-Élysées was raging. There were tricolor smoke bombs. French people from all walks of life, ages, and backgrounds were hugging each other. We were the champions—the soccer champions of the world! Those who were alive remember it. Those who were not dream about being there. Zinedine Zidane headed in two goals while Emmanuel Petit scored another on a counterattack in the game's ninety-third minute. France beat Brazil 3-0! Goalie Fabien Barthez fell to his knees in joy when the game ended; defensive midfielder Didier Deschamps kissed the championship cup; and Aimé Jacquet, the team's manager, was triumphantly carried off the field by his players. July 1, 1998 is a great day in France's history—perhaps even greater than when

France beat Croatia in the World Cup Final on July 15, 2018.

Everyone recalls where he was when France won in 1998. Some say the 1998 championship was a moment of national harmony that is rarely experienced. That night, there was no left-winger or right-winger. There was no Parisian or Marseilles resident. There was only a population proud of national victory, unified in joy with one heart. In moments like these, it is always surprising to see the sports press take up religious words—"the High Mass of soccer," the "Church of Maradona" (named after Diego Maradona, the famous Argentine soccer player), and the "hand of God." It's true there is incredible enthusiasm. Yet, this fervor only lasts for a short time. If only this feeling of national harmony could last longer than the ninety minutes of a game!

Someone may not be a soccer fan, and yet can have various other beautiful experiences, such as during a national feast, an opera, a family lunch, or the love a couple shares. The love of a couple is perhaps the most universal form of harmony, but it too has its limits. There is only one communion that is eternal—communion with our infinite God's love. Every man who is looking for the missing element in his life yearns for this love. We can look for it everywhere outside of ourselves.

But we can only experience true communion by responding to the inner divine call that comes from the depths of our hearts. Nobody wants to live in a permanent state of war with himself. To this end, we must overcome all the contradictions and inconsistencies that have shattered this harmony in our lives—with God, the world, and ourselves.

After the World Cup championship in 1998, the French projected onto the Arc de Triomphe, the famous war memorial in Paris, "The victory is in us. The victory is in us!" Yes, but the most beautiful victory is not won on a soccer field. It is played out in each of our hearts, in each of our souls. And Carlo, as a good Italian who was both a soccer player and fan, knew it! God Himself gives it to us when He lets us taste His victory over sin and death by being in communion with His love. He invites us to eat His Body and drink His Blood to grow and be in communion with His life. This is the first and most lovely of all the communions that we could desire. There are cups that shine, and there is a crown that does not fade. Carlo chased after that crown all his life: "Every athlete exercises self-control in all things. They do it to receive a perishable wreath, but we an imperishable. Well, I do not run aimlessly, I do not box as one beating the air, but I pommel my body and subdue it" (1 Cor. 9:25–27).

COMMUNION FIRST

We must go back a little in Carlo's life to understand this reality. Carlo's First Communion was not an isolated event in his life, but a union with God that he would be fed by day after day, an ever-deepening divine union that would orient his whole life as a child and adolescent. Carlo received his First Communion on June 16, 1998, the Tuesday after the Solemnity of Corpus Christi, the great feast on which Catholics worldwide celebrate with large Eucharistic processions the immense gift that Jesus gave us through the Eucharist.[25] One beautiful June day, his whole family traveled to the convent church of the hermit nuns of Sant'Ambrogio ad Nemus, with whom a priest friend of the Acutis family was familiar. It would become one of our young friend's favorite places. The convent, which is so beautiful and picturesque, is perched atop a rocky hill that overlooks the city of Varese, which is north of Milan. The view from the convent extends to the horizon of the surrounding hills. The landscape spreads out to the Alps, goes down to the lakes, and stretches toward a seemingly limitless plain. The sisters who live in the convent have a rare vocation, similar to life in the desert, given their general seclusion from the rest of the world. They are not

---

25. Corpus Christi is a feast that celebrates the gift of the Eucharist that Christ gave the Church. It takes place two weeks after Pentecost in the United States, and on the Thursday after Trinity Sunday in Rome. After many Eucharistic miracles, Pope Urban IV instituted this feast in 1264, asking St. Thomas Aquinas to write a whole liturgy, which includes the famous hymn "Pange Lingua": Sing, my tongue, the Saviour's glory, / Of His Flesh the mystery sing; / Of the Blood, all price exceeding, / Shed by our immortal King,/Destined, for the world's redemption, / From a noble womb to spring. / Centuries later, this hymn has gained millions of views on YouTube!

the first to live this way. They are following the model of their founders — Bl. Catarina and Bl. Juliana — who relied on the wisdom of St. Ambrose. He was the great bishop of Milan and a key figure in St. Augustine's conversion. For centuries, the life of these sisters has been a balance of prayer and work, solitude and communal life, and a sense of amazement before the marvels through which God manifests Himself in the beauty of nature and the value of each person they encounter. It is a life of joy and sacrifice. They pray according to the Ambrosian liturgy, an ancient rite named after the great saint. Those who come to pray with the sisters enter a timeless space, and to each man and woman they encounter on behalf of Christ, the sisters seek to give witness to His redeeming love in one way or another. Yet, these sisters live behind a grate in their enclosure in rarely interrupted silence, far from Milan's noise. Why are they so far away from the world? To live only for God — in prayer, in their consecrated love as members of a religious community, and in the hospitality they offer to all who visit. That day in June 1998, they welcomed a pilgrim they still remember. Carlo experienced one of the most beautiful days of his life, his First Communion, as he wore his white alb and white shoes, along with his wooden cross around his neck. It was a day for which he had waited so long. He was only seven years old. This can seem very young. But, as we say, it is the age of reason. Carlo experienced this big step because he was driven by an immense desire to know

Jesus and receive Him in his heart. That day, for the first time, the little child was the first one to enter into the central aisle to receive Him who would become his heart's life. These Latin words are engraved on the tabernacle of the convent's church: Omnia Christus est nobis — "Christ is everything for us." We should make this a motto for our own lives. That day, Carlo was ecstatic when he received the "bread of angels," as the "Panis Angelicus," composed by St. Thomas Aquinas, refers to the Eucharist. This hymn is sung every year on Corpus Christi: "The bread of angels becomes bread of men. The heavenly bread puts an end to appearances. Oh, wonderful mystery: the humble and poor servant nourishes himself on his Lord!" This day, Carlo was the humble one for the first time.

The story of Carlo's sacraments included many chapters in the young boy's life. It included his Baptism, by which he entered into the life of the Church and God Himself and his First Communion, which would become his highway to Heaven and which he would receive faithfully every day. He also frequently received the Sacrament of Reconciliation. We will speak about that again later. Finally, the Sacrament of Anointing of the Sick gave him strength to go to the end of the road. There were only two sacraments he did not receive — Holy Orders, in which a man is ordained a deacon, priest, or bishop; and marriage, in which one becomes a spouse. How would Carlo have discerned his path had he lived longer? What would have been his vocation? Would he have been a zealous priest or a devoted husband and father? Regardless of the answer, Carlo did not wait years to respond to the call he received at Baptism. It was the call of being a part of a holy people dedicated to the Lord. Carlo's vocation would be one of simple holiness and a daily consecration to God. He was not going to wait for big signs or until he could engage in extraordinary adventures. Instead, Carlo would find joy in ordinary things. He could have been an "average Catholic." He could have dreamed about a life of extraordinary holiness, about saints who did not resemble him, and ultimately have regretted his more ordinary life, a life in which he lived in a city that was neither too big nor too small, and in a family that was neither too poor nor too rich. In short, he could have been a middle-of-the-road, lukewarm Catholic. Instead, in modern, conventional society, he was able to pursue all of his originality by responding to the call of holiness, which is a unique call for everyone.

THE EUCHARIST, HIS SCHOOL OF LOVE

But what did Carlo find so attractive in the Eucharist that he went to daily Mass? How did he keep the desire that burned as hotly as it did on the day of his First Communion – a love that was as vivid as on the day of his first encounter? In reality, Carlo did not believe there was a second Communion. There was only a First Communion, to which he wanted to adhere his whole life. His school of life would be the Eucharist. He had found his best model on how to live. Where? In front of the Blessed Sacrament, he learned to look at the world with God's eyes. With God's gaze, Carlo enlarged his own horizon and left his comfort zone. He learned to move toward others and become more farsighted. Carlo often said, "The Eucharist is my highway to to Heaven," when asked what attracted him so much to churches. His parish priest recalls this well. When he saw this young man moving forward to receive Communion, he saw a young man approaching the Eucharist as the greatest gift of God's love. Carlo knew the Eucharist is God, who sees humanity's sufferings. His friends were struck by the way Carlo participated in Mass, even during the week. Sometimes, they went there simply to accompany him. Carlo's devotion and attention contrasted with their distraction, which prevented them from really understanding what was going on during Mass. His friends were surprised to see him kneeling and listening to the priest's words with the same intensity every day. Was it possible that God was truly present in this church? Was it possible to believe in the Real Presence of the Eucharist? Yes, and Carlo showed them the way, witnessing that God's presence in this world was not just an image. Carlo had a simple heart. He also knew that Jesus was acquainted with His disciples' simplicity. He knew that there were believers who took everything literally and sometimes did not pay attention to the deeper meaning contained in each word. But when Jesus spoke in parables, He also spoke about Heaven in simple terms. Infinity is our homeland. Heaven has been waiting for us for all eternity.

In order to live life as passionately as he did, Carlo had a little secret. He said: "My secret is to contact Jesus every day," which he principally did by participating in daily Mass, beginning with First Communion forward. It didn't matter if a church wasn't the prettiest, or a priest didn't preach the best homily, or those leading the liturgy were boring. Only one thing mattered to Carlo. God was there. His secret was not insignificant, but available to everyone: "We have all been created with the potential to be saints. But God also made us free—free to do good as well as evil. I want to follow the example of John the Apostle, the beloved disciple. Each one of us can become a beloved disciple of Jesus, as John was."

What impressed him, what he wanted to most imitate in St. John, was that John accompanied Jesus to the Cross, whereas all His other Apostles fled. John was also the one who leaned on Jesus' heart during the Last Supper. Carlo thought that it was the most beautiful image of what a Christian should be. All his life, Carlo had this heart-to-heart relationship with Jesus. He wanted, like St. John, to become Jesus' friend. Participating in Mass was going to the foot of the Cross with St. John. It was going where nobody wanted to go and staying with the one who loves us most.

For Carlo, going to church daily meant getting on "the highway to Heaven." A providential wink made this image become even more alive for Carlo. The first highway that was built in the world is the one that linked Milan, where Carlo lived, to Varese, the city where he made his First Communion. This project, which was completed in 1924, was a real futuristic project aimed at connecting two cities in a way that was more certain, direct, and efficient. At the beginning of the third millennium, Providence wanted Carlo to take this highway known as "the Lakes Expressway" to open up a new highway for the third millennium — the highway to Heaven.

SACRAMENTUM ADMORIS

Carlo said: "Soon, we will be saints!" But then, to be a saint, is it enough to go to Mass? Of course not! However, living in God's presence remains the surest path. Carlo read about the stories of great saints and discovered the central place prayer had in their lives. He saw the determining role God's love played in their holiness, how the sacrament of God's love is indeed the Eucharist. According to our young friend, we can sometimes experience such a communion with God that this time should not be sacrificed. This was particularly the case with the Mass, where Carlo felt such a strong intimacy with Jesus that he wanted only one thing. It was to encourage all his friends to experience 200 percent of this silence and meditation. St. Teresa of Avila said that the times of communion with God that we can experience in prayer allow us to be instructed by Him. Another mystic that Carlo really liked, St. Mary Magdalene de' Pazzi, loved to repeat that moments of intimate communion with God are the most precious times we can have in our earthly existence. They are profound moments in which we can talk with God and let ourselves be inflamed by His love. During these most intimate times, we do not need books or human teachers, because Jesus becomes our only teacher. He is the one who teaches us to love. In fact, the Eucharist is the sacrament of God's love. Jesus teaches us, "Greater love has no man than this, that a man lay down his life for his friends" (John 15:13). This is exactly what Jesus does for us in the Eucharist. He gives us His life. He gives us His Body and Blood, so that we can live and love like Him. In one of his meditations, Carlo wrote: "Jesus is love, and the more that we feed on Him, the more we increase our ability to love." This is not just a pious wish. Carlo's devotion did not make him a "church lady," or a less flawed Christian. His life was consistent. Carlo did not act like an angel kneeling in church, only to become a beast when he left. He knew that to grow in God's love and the Eucharist without growing in the love of his brothers would be to become a Pharisee in modern times.

He found his model in the Eucharistic Jesus by seeing his God, who offered Himself to Carlo in such a poor and

vulnerable form. Thus, while growing up, Carlo looked for
all kinds of volunteer opportunities to serve. One year, on
his birthday, his grandparents gave him games that he didn't
really want. So, Carlo visited the Capuchins in Milan, who
served more than 5,000 meals per day to the needy, and he
offered these games to the poor children who had none. He
also joined a team of volunteers who helped the Capuchins
in serving these meals. In the process, Carlo was blessed to
meet Fr. Giulio Savoldi, a sort of Padre Pio from northern
Italy, who became a true model for Carlo. This priest took up
the mission of Br. Cecilo Cortinovis, who died in 1984. Br.
Cecilo was a Capuchin particularly committed to serving the
poor. The Capuchin brother also hid many Jews and political opponents in his monastery during the Second World
War, and he assisted those wounded and families impacted
by the bombings. Carlo wanted to emulate these great spiritual men of God, who also knew how to be servants of
men. Every night, Carlo asked his grandmother to prepare
a snack for a beggar who lived in a public garden not far
from their home. When he dropped it off, Carlo also gave
the poor man a euro from his own pocket money, so that
the man could buy some coffee in the morning. His grandmother Luana said: "Carlo liked to talk to those who begged
at the church exit. When he saw others suffer, he clearly
suffered with them."

Incidentally, Carlo's zeal was, at times, a little too much
for his parents! His desire to go to church every day surprised

them as well, but they respected it. On the other hand, his progressive detachment from material goods aggravated them at times. When his mother took him shopping one day, she offered to buy him a new pair of shoes. But Carlo, being enamored with Franciscan poverty, declined her offer, for his shoes were still in good condition: "Mom, one pair is enough for me."

TO ADORE GOD ALWAYS AND AT ALL TIMES

After his First Communion, Carlo spent increasing time silently adoring God in various churches. While people spend hours under the sun to get a tan, Carlo knew that "tanning of our souls" in front of the "Eucharistic Sun" is a much better use of our time: "Under the sun, we end up getting a tan," he said. "Under the Eucharistic Jesus' gaze, we become holy!" Carlo grew in his love for Christ through regular adoration. On his daily hikes, Carlo appreciated the beauty of nature, yet he knew, even though God's immensity is present in nature, that we do not encounter Him by touching a tree or looking at a mountain. We encounter God by adoring His personal and loving presence in His sacraments, sacred rituals that still resonate 2,000 years after the Resurrection. Carlo understood that God's presence is not in noise or commotion, but in the silence of the Church—this place where God is adored. Successive popes have written encyclicals and other documents exhorting Christians to have a stronger faith in Christ's Real Presence in the Eucharist. Carlo really liked Pope St. John Paul II. He read his encyclical where he defined the Church as the place where the Eucharist is.[26] There, Carlo discovered a greater love for the Eucharistic Jesus, who is perpetually present in the Church. This implies that He must be perpetually adored by those who love Him. Pope St. John Paul II experienced some awful years under the domination of atheistic Communism in Poland, his native land. He saw the harmful and fatal consequences of a totalitarian government that wanted to control men to the point of removing their freedom of conscience and religious liberty. These consequences reach beyond the boundaries of Communism. The pope saw that atheistic humanism wished to reduce the Church to a friendly gathering of men and women who share good values. The Church is more than a meeting place for men and women to hold each other's hands. For St. John Paul II, this conviviality had

---

26. *Ecclesia de Eucharistia* (The Church [lives] from the Eucharist) was John Paul II's last encyclical, which he issued on Holy Thursday in 2003 (April 17). It recalls the link between the institution of the Eucharist and the priesthood. Popes have traditionally issued a message of encouragement to priests on Holy Thursday, and this encyclical is part of the heritage John Paul II wanted to leave Christians giving witness in the twenty-first century. It forms a trilogy with *Novo millennio ineunte* (At the beginning of the new millennium), which invites us to look at the new millennium as an opportunity to advance the New Evangelization, and *Rosarium Virginis Mariae* (The Rosary of the Virgin Mary), in which the pontiff proposes that we view Mary as a model to encounter Christ anew by meditating on the mysteries of his life in praying the Rosary.

to be transfigured by the presence of the Risen One in the midst of believers. But how does God make Himself present in our world today?

For centuries, the Israelites implored God to show them His face: "Let thy face shine, that we may be saved!" (Ps. 80:3). They longed to see God face-to-face, to speak to Him, and adore Him. When God became man, He showed us the face that was to save us, which is Christ Himself. Carlo was, incidentally, profoundly impressed by the enthusiasm with which the orthodox faithful venerated the icons of Christ the Redeemer during his trip to the Meteora in Greece. By kissing a representation of the Savior's face, they seemed to make themselves present, through faith, to a reality that went far beyond the icon's materiality. What are we to say, then, of Christ's presence that we adore and receive in the Eucharist? It goes far beyond the visible matter of the bread and wine! What a mystery that such a powerful God, the Creator of Heaven and earth, chose to manifest Himself in our fragile humanity and left us with the simplest signs to speak to us about His unique presence among us! God did not reveal Himself in Christ in power, but in the weakness of crucified hands. This presence is so great that it drives us to worship. We are in the presence of a great mystery as Christ's very words resonate in our churches. It is even greater than the mystery of the bush that burned without being consumed, which Moses encountered on Mount Horeb. Like the angels in the book of Revelation that fall on their faces before the one who is seated on His Heavenly throne (Rev. 7:11), we too are called to bow down before this immense presence of God. Our incense, hymns, the splendor of our altars turn our attention to the One who is coming. The Eucharist makes present on earth the glory God wishes to reveal to us in Eternity. In the Gospel of John, Jesus gave this extraordinary response: "The hour is coming, and is now here, when the true worshipers will worship the Father in spirit and truth, for the Father seeks such as these to worship him" (John 4:23). Jesus gave everyone the opportunity to adore God everywhere — not in His absence, but in His presence. By making Himself man, God intermingled the mystery of His divinity with the humility of our humanity, and left us with His Body and Blood, His Soul and Divinity, His Spirit and His Truth, so that we can adore Him everywhere and at all times. In fact, in each Mass that is celebrated, the Church can once again connect with Christ's sacrifice in every consecrated host. Adoring God is not putting Him in a box and going into a mystical trance. It is returning to the foot of the Cross like St. John in Jerusalem. It is finding Heaven already on earth and placing ourselves in the mystery of His presence and joining Him in His offering of love.

One day, Carlo's father proposed that they go on an extraordinary trip to the Holy Land in Jerusalem. We know how much Carlo liked to travel. But the son answered his father by saying: "Dad, I prefer to stay in Milan, when I think that Jesus makes Himself present here. Why go where Jesus was 2,000 years ago, whereas He is here now?"

The truth is, Carlo dreamed about going on this big trip because he really enjoyed the adventure. But when he observed the extent to which the churches in Milan were abandoned, Carlo said he preferred to go on a pilgrimage to each of his city's churches. The fact that we are ready to travel several hundred miles, whereas we are not ready to go only a few miles to pray to God, wounded him. This is why, when he traveled, the first thing that Carlo looked for was an open church to pray and stand close to the tabernacle, where Jesus' Real Presence rested.

As we have noted earlier, Carlo did not keep a diary. Like many great saints, he never talked about himself. But what is left of his writings, besides his class notebooks, are his meditations. Carlo did not leave us with beautiful Eucharistic hymns like St. Thomas Aquinas, but his meditations say a lot about the depth of his adoration. It is very tempting to think that meditation is reserved for monks. It is difficult to keep praying. Distractions, worries, and doubts can discourage us and convince us that we do not know how to adore — as if we had to be balanced at the top of a column like Stylite monks! For Carlo, meditating was not rocket science. Carlo always had a lot of things going on in his head. Like many of us, he found it difficult not to be distracted in his prayer. He often talked about it with his priest friends, from whom he sought advice on praying. Yet, shortly before he died, Carlo noted his progress to his spiritual father in Bologna: "I see that the more I love Jesus, the less distracted I am. Now, I want to love Him completely."

Carlo knew he could commune with God in every moment and every place that God made Himself present. He knew that meditation was not merely a breathing technique or a simple self-awareness exercise. The most beautiful meditation is to make yourself present before this Real Presence of God in the Eucharist in order to "adore the Body and Blood of our Lord Jesus Christ, who is really present as He was when Jesus lived in Palestine." Significantly, the stand upon which the monstrance is placed during Eucharistic Adoration is called a "tabor." Mount Tabor is the mountain where Jesus was transfigured and revealed His glory to Peter, James, and John. Peter wanted to set up three tents so as to remain in the presence of God's glory at all times on Mount Tabor. The tabor is where Carlo wanted to spend his life, in the presence of God's glory. Yet, he was well aware that the world was not always a monstrance of precious stones to welcome God's presence. Often, there is not much room in our lives to welcome God or much time to adore Him. In one of his notes, he said:

> Jesus made Himself man by taking on the flesh of a young woman who was barely fifteen years old. She is the one whom He chose to be His mother. Likewise, He chose a poor carpenter as His adoptive father.

When he was born, they were rejected by all those who refused to accommodate them. They found only a stable to shelter them. When we think about it, to be welcomed in a poor stable in Bethlehem was still better than to be welcomed in a house where He was not wanted. Even if it was squalid, the barn knew how to be more welcoming in a dignified manner than all the beautiful homes that did not know how to make room for Him. It's just amazing to me that God chose poverty rather than richness!

Carlo really knew that the stable was his childlike heart, which is the heart of a true adorer.

RICARDO AND SIMONE

Carlo's faith in God's presence makes us want to ask: How did he do it? Carlo was often overwhelmed by his friends' questions, particularly about the Eucharist, his favorite subject. Yet, this is not a subject that children talk about much, let alone comfortably. But Carlo so easily found the right words that his counsel became featured in a cartoon that included two of his friends, Ricardo and Simone, who spoke to Carlo about the Eucharist. His explanations about the Mass are still used today for catechism classes in Italy. Ricardo asked: "But how can we be certain that Jesus intended to leave us His Body?" Later, Simone wondered,

"Why do we maintain that the Last Supper speaks realistically about His Body and Blood, whereas it was seemingly not referenced to before then?" Carlo took all these questions very seriously, because he had first pondered these questions himself. When Carlo had doubts about his faith, he talked them over with his mother and priests.

But, above all, he loved rereading the Gospel according to John, which he knew almost by heart since he had looked it over so thoroughly. He especially loved Christ's Bread of Life Discourse in John 6. Jesus was preparing His disciples to experience a great mystery: "I am the living bread which came down from heaven" (John 6:51). When Carlo talked about this passage from the Gospel, it was as if he were reliving it. It was like a play. He took up Jesus' word. Then, without stage directions, he talked about what his contemporaries were thinking in their hearts. How is it possible that this man can give us His flesh to eat? Who does He think He is when He says, "he will have eternal life and I will raise them up on the last day" (John 6:54). His friends asked him: But how can we be sure that those are His real words?—Do you really believe it?—Yes, Carlo replied, with a bewildering sense of confidence. Jesus was very serious. He said it and repeated it: "I am the living bread which came down from heaven." When Carlo talked about the Gospel, he appealed to his friends: "But if you are also hungry and thirsty, do not be satisfied with words. If you are thirsty and hungry for Jesus, really believe that

He will feed you today. He is the one we must look for, and not only the miracles that surprise us."

When he talked about the Gospel, Carlo did not hesitate to use simple words that his friends could understand. He told them that "Jesus is not afraid of being rejected." He preferred remaining faithful to the truth rather than changing a single Word of His Father's. He explained: "Jesus is, in fact, rather nice. When His contemporaries did not understand Him, rather than telling them that they did not understand anything, he preferred to repeat it for them again."

Carlo's friends admitted to him that, very often, they were bored in church, and that they went to Holy Communion simply because everyone else was. They felt as if they had lost their childhood faith—the faith of their First Communion. Now that they were older, they found it harder to believe what their parents or catechists told them. When they went to Holy Communion, they thought only of one thing: the soccer game planned after Mass. They felt the Faith was difficult to believe when people started to develop a scientific mind. Carlo shared their questions and doubts. But he knew that it was possible to find answers. He recalled from Scripture, "Always be prepared to make a defense to anyone who calls you to account for the hope that is in you" (1 Pet. 3:15), Carlo's research was so thorough that his knowledge impressed not only his friends, but also his parents, who did not know as much about the

Faith as their son did. According to Carlo, to be in communion with God, you had to have, above all, a lot of humility
and a strong faith. He knew that you had to imitate Mary
during the Annunciation, who said she was only the Lord's
humble servant. Carlo knew that we had to become like
her—the living tabernacle of God's presence in the world.

THE MIRACLES OF FAITH

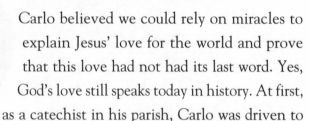

Carlo believed we could rely on miracles to
explain Jesus' love for the world and prove
that this love had not had its last word. Yes,
God's love still speaks today in history. At first,
as a catechist in his parish, Carlo was driven to
find new and better ways to share the Catholic Faith with
young people. We should start by explaining that youth
catechism classes in Italy were not typically handled by
"catechism ladies," but, more often, young team leaders
in youth groups. At the beginning of the week, the team
leaders would receive instruction on a particular topic from
their pastor or another adult in the parish, and then present
the lesson to their classes. Carlo became a catechist when he
was twelve, and he would serve in that role for three and a
half years. He saw that children in catechism class were not
interested when you only spoke about the Faith in abstract
terms. It was from this understanding that Carlo would
find new ways to share the gospel, particularly through the
creation of an exhibition and the development of websites.

Carlo was especially fascinated by Eucharistic miracles. He thought they were a key way to help us understand what happens at Mass. Jesus told us: "I am with you always, to the close of the age" (Matt. 28:20). Carlo, who loved the Eucharist, thought that it was obvious that Christ was truly present at Mass. This presence also manifested itself through the extraordinary signs that are Eucharist miracles. Far from occurring only the Middle Ages, many Eucharistic miracles took place during the twenty-first century, as recently as 2006, 2008, and even in 2013, after Carlo's death. Eucharistic miracles are rare, yet Carlo knew they clearly bear witness to what happens on our altars every day at Mass. The miracles are extraordinary and prodigious signs that help our faith. The "hidden" Jesus, as the little shepherds of Fatima said, reveals Himself through a tremendous sign. This is what happened around the year 750 in Lanciano, Italy. A Basilian monk doubted that God could make Himself present in the Blessed Sacrament. He celebrated Mass indifferently. Then, suddenly, he saw the consecrated host transform itself into flesh and the wine into blood. Everyone saw this. It is still the case today when you go on a pilgrimage there. Every pilgrim can still see the miraculous species. They have been aged by time, but they continue to be kept in a beautiful reliquary in the ancient Church of Saints Legontian and Domitian, now known as the Church of Saint Francis of the Miracle. The miracle did not stop there. In 1970, in response to critics, the bishop of Lanciano had scientific analyses of the miraculous relics carried out. Dr. Edoardo Linoli, who was the director of the hospital in Arezzo, Italy, and a professor of anatomy, histology,[27] chemistry, and clinical microscopy, led the investigation. His findings, which were announced on March 4, 1971, were dramatic. The relics were genuine muscular tissue of the myocardium, i.e., the human heart, and also hardened portions of real human blood. The miraculous blood belonged to the same AB blood group as the sample taken from the Shroud of Turin, which is believed to be the burial cloth of Jesus. The blood analysis also revealed seric proteins that correspond to fresh blood, whereas this miracle took place more than 1,200 years ago. And yet the blood had not been mixed with any other substance, which could have altered its content through the centuries. This research so perplexed the international medical community, which was skeptical and disbelieving, that the World Health Organization's Superior Council went so far as to launch its own independent investigation. It published a report in December 1976 in New York and Geneva, confirming that the phenomenon could not be scientifically explained. This miracle tested not only science, therefore, but also faith. On November 3, 1974, even before his election as pope, the future St. John Paul II went on a pilgrimage to Lanciano to

---

27. A branch of biology that is concerned with the structure of living tissues.

see what some thought was an old relic of the past. But Carlo believed that this discovery was to be the start of extensive research on other Eucharistic miracles. Some such miracles are well-known, like the one in Bolsena in 1263, which is at the root of the Corpus Christi feast that was mentioned at the beginning of this chapter. Others are almost unknown. There have even been some in France—in Avignon in 1433 or Bordeaux in 1822, in Dijon in 1430, or Douai in 1254, in La Rochelle in 1461, and even in Paris in 1290. These were in such different places, at such distant times, and yet even in our present time …

How could we not talk about an extraordinary miracle that the future Pope Francis was privileged to witness while Carlo was alive? At the time, Jorge Mario Bergoglio was the archbishop of Buenos Aires. Three surprising events in Saint Mary Church in Almagro caused the future pope to call on Professor Ricardo Castañon Gomez to investigate them. During the children's Mass on July 24, 1994, while the priest was going to the tabernacle for consecrated hosts, he saw a drop of blood flowing along the side of the ciborium. This event would be recognized as a Eucharistic miracle by the future Pope Francis. Professor Gomez specialized in these phenomena. His response was always the same: "Let us not stop being amazed!" In fact, each time these miracles occurred, there was also resistance or disbelief. It is not easy to believe when one is a monk celebrating Mass every day, and who almost gets tired of God's presence. It is not easy to believe when we celebrate Mass for dozens of distracted children and feel we are the only one following what is going on. These miracles come to awaken our faith. Carlo understood this. Today, thanks to him and the website www.miracolieucaristici.org, which he developed, thousands of people have heard about these signs. But how are these miracles to be explained? After a Eucharistic miracle in Bolsena, St. Thomas Aquinas would explain, at the pope's request, what really takes place in a Eucharistic miracle so as to convince skeptics and calm eccentrics: this is not about chasing after miracles. On the contrary, Eucharistic miracles open our eyes to the permanent miracle. If Christ rose from the dead and ascended to Heaven, and if He is seated at the right hand of the Father as the Creed tells us, what should we think of a Eucharistic miracle? What is it? This is the question that the Hebrews asked in the desert when they saw the manna falling from the sky: Man ou? In Hebrew, this means "what is it?"

There are two people on earth whose relics will never be found—Jesus and Mary. Both have already entered into the glory of Heaven, body and soul. Thus, people do not talk about Jesus' relics in Buenos Aires or Lanciano, but about the relics of the miracle. In the face of our unbelief, the Lord can give us signs that awaken our faith and understanding. Eucharistic miracles, therefore, are the sign of an extraordinary act. Finally, what do these Eucharistic miracles tell us? The Eucharist is not to be taken lightly. It is, without fail, an extraordinary event. Jesus really offered us His Body and Blood to save us and to receive life from His life. And so, why do these Eucharistic miracles occur? Jesus said to the paralytic: "'So that you may know that the Son of Man has authority on earth to forgive sins'—he said to the paralytic—'I say to you, stand up, take your mat and go to your home'" (Mark 2:10–11). Jesus performed a miracle in our physical reality to make us enter into His spiritual power with a stronger faith. So, in order for us to know that the Son of Man has the power to be present in the Eucharist, we witness Eucharistic miracles. These miracles, like the miraculous healings in Lourdes, follow the miracles that Jesus performed during His life on earth to heal and save men. To explain them, St. Thomas Aquinas said that, in these miracles, the appearance changes, whereas, in the Eucharist, the substance does. Eucharistic miracles are an extraordinary transformation that speaks to us of a much greater and deeper miracle that occurs in a more common way—transubstantiation.[28] Eucharistic miracles, in particular, place us in the presence of Flesh and Blood that are, for us, a witness of Christ's sacrifice. The Eucharist really puts us in the very presence of the most important moment of

---

28. Since an important meeting of bishops in Rome, the Fourth Lateran Council in 1215, the Catholic Church has used this term to describe the Eucharistic mystery. The idea was to avoid misconceptions about the Eucharist, misconceptions that described Jesus as not truly present or, on the contrary, that we could objectify Him. Christ's presence is both real and mystical.

Christ's life and sacrifice on the Cross. Nobody can explain it better than Carlo did in his exhibition:

> Jerusalem is in each church. Why be discouraged? God is always with us, and He will never abandon us. But how can we understand this truth? There are so many people who are ready to get into interminable lines to attend a concert or soccer game. Yet, I have a hard time seeing the same lines in our church entrances. The whole world could meet Jesus there. Let us think about it. This is serious! Jesus is physically present in our midst as He was with His disciples while He was alive. Let us not leave the one who comes to help and support us on our earthly path on His own.

DESECRATED CHARITY

Of all the virtues, the one that we have most misused is, undoubtedly, charity. We have reduced charity to something that we do — icing on the cake of the "nice Catholic," who gives a dollar to the collection and his spare change to the poor person asking for help. We have sugarcoated charity, just as we have sugarcoated love. We have reduced both to something that we must *do*, whereas it is not so much a question of *doing* as of *dwelling*. Jesus never asked us to *do* charity no more than to *do* love. But He told us: "Abide [dwell] in my love" (John 15:9).

More than that, charity has been desecrated as one dese-
crates a church, because we have reduced Christ's love to
a love that is ordinary and purely horizontal. Christian
charity is not simply a charitable activity. Christian charity
is really God who loves the world in His Body, which is the
Church. This is why we talk about charity as a theological
virtue—that is to say, a virtue through which man cannot
act without God. The beginning and end of charity is God
and, consequently, we can also love man, the creature God
created and saved because He loved mankind first. Charity
is truly the virtue through which we love God above everything for Himself and our neighbor as ourselves for the love
of God. That is why, if we had to attach a virtue to the
Sacrament of the Eucharist, it would have to be charity.
Charity, like the Eucharist, must transfigure the Christian's
whole life, as it transformed Carlo's life.

St. Paul said that if "[I] do not have love, I am nothing"
(1 Cor. 13:2). We can say the same about Carlo's life without
the Eucharist. The Eucharist is, above all, God who loves us
in His Church and invites us to live from His charity. On
the evening of the Last Supper, before offering Himself on
the Cross, Jesus offered Himself to His brothers, through
unambiguous words: "This is my body which is given for you"
(Luke 22:19). These words of Christ transformed Carlo's
life. The Eucharist is God's love given to men so that they
could live from His love, love Him, and love each other as
He loved us. Carlo said: "When we are in communion with

God, we are in communion with a love that is catching. As we are loved by Him, we can, in this way, love the world." This love will never go away.

THE WORD OF GOD

Truly, truly, I say to you, he who believes has eternal life. I am the bread of life. Your fathers ate the manna in the wilderness, and they died. This is the bread which comes down from heaven, that a man may eat of it and not die. I am the living bread which came down from heaven; if any one eats of this bread, he will live for ever; and the bread which I shall give for the life of the world is my flesh. (John 6:47–51)

LIFE QUESTIONS

➤ When did I make my First Communion? When I receive Communion, do I try to experience this event as a new "First Communion" to understand more about the greatness of what is happening?

➤ In my life, do I see the link between loving God and loving my neighbor?

➤ How do I prepare myself to receive the Body and Blood of Christ in the Blessed Sacrament?

➤ What or who is my model of love?

➤ What am I ready to do for the love of God?

PRAYER TO GOD

My God, I love you with all my heart, above all, because You are infinitely good, and I want to love my neighbor as myself out of love for You.

Chapter 5
Missionary 2.0

THE NEW DIGITAL FRONTIER

How did Europeans view the earth before they discovered America? If this discovery changed the world's face, a new but very different "frontier" disrupted our lives at the beginning of the third millennium. Discovery is no longer about great navigational expeditions, like the pioneers who discovered America, from the Atlantic coast to the Pacific Ocean. It is about a new, limitless land called the digital frontier. Carlo's contemporaries can recall it well. They saw the old Minitel, which was once the world's most successful online service, get ousted by the World Wide Web and Microsoft Windows 95, which people increasingly used to access the Internet through home computers that became common. Then, Windows 98 made a big splash around the world. Apple Macs, which PCs overshadowed for a while, also took part in this technological race, becoming increasingly sophisticated and more efficient. Portable consoles also successively appeared. The first one was Game Boy in 1992, with its little black-and-white screen, directional cross, and two red buttons. Game Boy Color followed in 1998, and, finally, Game Boy Advance in 2001. Let's not forget consoles like Sega or Nintendo 64, and, of course, PlayStation with its four buttons on the front: the green triangle, pink square, red circle, and blue x.

Cell phones also appeared in our lives. At the beginning of the '90s, they were reserved for soldiers and heads of companies. They looked more like enormous walkie-talkies. In 1999, though, a new cell phone initiated a revolution. It was the Nokia 3210, which had a built-in antenna. Today, this is a feature we take for granted. But a couple of decades ago, it was a major innovation. Up until then, cell phones did not fit into any pocket. Today, we can't even part with them. In short, the digital frontier expanded quickly and enormously, opening its doors to a new market. It completely changed our habits. In the past, to get the weather forecast, you had to wait for radio updates or the local TV news, unless severe weather was on the way. Today, all you have to do is open the designated application on your cell. In the past, a phone call from one country to another was a luxury. Today, we can now easily talk to each other in a video conference to check up on the family. In the past, it took days or weeks to get our photos developed. Today, with just a few clicks, we can shoot and share them with friends across of the world. This virtual platform, the Internet, caused the physical boundaries that separated different countries and continents to fall overnight. It made an extraordinary amount of information accessible to everyone everywhere (provided you had a network connection). People dreamed about it. The Jesuit Pierre Teilhard de Chardin alluded to the emergence of a "noosphere" at the beginning of the twentieth century. It was a network of knowledge that would unite the whole world. Wikipedia is in the process of achieving this vision.

But is there a place for God on this new frontier? How can we, for that matter, live out our faith online? Wikipedia provided an article on Jesus in the winter of 2001, during the online encyclopedia's first months. It was written by Jimbo Wales, also known as Jimmy Wales, Wikipedia's founder. Though Jesus did not delay in appearing on Wikipedia, the fact remains that the article offers us only a historical person. Carlo and all Christians know Jesus is much more than that. So, who dares talk about the living Christ on the Internet?

A MISSIONARY HEART

To understand how Carlo would respond to this question, we have to wonder what could have awakened a missionary desire in his heart. Many events fueled this momentum. One day a Jesuit chaplain came into Carlo's classroom and suggested that the students create little Christian fraternities — also known as Communities of Christian Life (CCL) — in the high school. He invited the young people to discover Ignatian spirituality.[29] The idea was to meet and meditate on God's Word by immersing themselves in Jesus' life. "Who would like to participate in this project?" The chaplain was full of hope when he asked the question in Carlo's eighth-grade classroom. There was a big pause. The surprised priest asked himself, "Did they not understand the offer, or do they simply not want to participate?" The only one interested was Carlo, who was looking for a more fraternal life with his fellow students. Unfortunately, the priest's offer would not lead to anything because of a lack of interest.

Another time, a missionary returned from China to address Carlo and his classmates on the foreign missions. Christians have experienced terrible oppression in Communist China. Yet, while this elderly missionary talked about his incredible memories and the complex situation of the Church in China, most of the middle-schoolers kept talking. They were sadly not interested in what he was telling them, to such an extent that those who wanted to listen, like Carlo, could not. Carlo had a lot of questions to ask. This mission at the other end of world fascinated

---

29. Saint Ignatius of Loyola, the founder of the Jesuits and Ignatian spirituality, was a great Church reformer. His spirituality, which meditates on the life of Jesus, invites every Christian to immerse himself in the moments of Jesus' life, and to place himself in the same frame of mind to discern the choices in his own life.

him. How do you transmit God's love? How do the Chinese view Jesus? How do you become a missionary? There were such important questions to which Carlo would probably not get complete answers during his life on earth. But they became practical realities in his daily life. Without ever going to the other side of the world, he burned with this missionary flame that compelled him to introduce Jesus to all those he met. But he was going to develop his mission on a completely new frontier, which was the digital frontier. He would expend so much effort that, one day, his grandmother told him, "But Carlo, being a missionary is for the priest! It is not up to you to do all that!" Carlo would reply, "But, Nonna, the priest does not know how to do all that. And, besides, with all that he has to do in church and all the people he has to meet, he does not have the time. So, this mission is for me."

THE GEEK

We have noted several times that computer science fascinated Carlo. At a time when turnkey sites like WordPress did not yet exist, he spent a lot of time coding new computer programs, making calculations, and writing mathematical formulas that nobody around him could understand. His friends were always happy to learn from him, though, and Carlo was quite happy to share his progress and computer discoveries. One day, one of his friends came pleading for help. She was upset, because she could no longer access her computer. In fact, she had forgotten her password. Carlo, who could dexterously manipulate the MS-DOS interface, unlocked her computer in no time. But his talents were not only used to resolve little problems. He also knew how to use them for a bigger cause. When he was fourteen, his parish priest asked him to develop the website for the Church of Santa Maria Segreta in Milan. Carlo knew the parish well, as we indicated earlier, because he was already serving as a team leader in their youth group. During the week, he helped prepare children for Confirmation.[30] Carlo was a fantastic catechist. He loved to find the right words to reach young people about the greatness of God's love. And he fruitfully combined his missionary zeal with his passion for computer science to create his parish's website. At the time, this project was really innovative. YouTube did not even exist. Carlo was part of the first-generation of online missionaries who did not have any hang-ups about using technological tools and computer science in the service of a spiritual and religious cause. He was a pioneer and an explorer of this new frontier that is the Internet, which was still in its infancy at the dawn of the third millennium.

The Catholic Church was lagging behind online, though. Few parishes had a website at this time. Some Christians were trailblazers in this field, like Fr. Roberto Busa, S.J.,

---

30. In Italy, people are usually confirmed around the age of twelve.

who met Thomas J. Watson, the man who made IBM into a global brand, in 1949. Father Busa persuaded Watson to fund the digitizing of all the Latin works of St. Thomas Aquinas. By 1989, this Jesuit mathematician and theologian released a CD-ROM that could search all that Aquinas had written. In 2005, Father Busa put this compendium on the Internet, making it one of the first examples of hypertext, better known as an online "link."

In France, the first Catholics to launch into the online adventure were young people, who, in December 2000, set up a website called ChristiCity. It became the "City of Jesus," an early Internet Christian community. Matthieu Grimpret, the founder of ChristiCity, told the *Le Monde* newspaper in 2001, "The concept of a community, which is at the heart of the Internet, is also at the heart of the Catholic Church. We felt that there was an interesting parallel." After World Youth Day in Paris in 1997, where he observed the increasing number of young people attracted to the Faith, Grimpret joined other young entrepreneurs to establish ChristiCity, so they could offer "doctrinal and spiritual content" that would be both "dynamic and interactive." The website speaks to young people about Jesus where they are at and in words that resonate with them. They were Internet missionaries from the outset.

In Carlo's case, he was not a great theologian or associated with a group of young professionals. He was merely a fourteen-year-old adolescent entrusted with setting up the

website for his parish, which was one of the most promi-
nent parishes in the Italian economic capital. Thus, a great
responsibility was given to him. It was not a trivial venture.
All you have to do is see what this site has become. In
addition, the parish can now boast that they entered the
online world of evangelization through the hands of a
boy whom the pope has since beatified! The website has
kept the same spirit of clarity and simplicity that Carlo
tried to give it.

After this online achievement, other institutions
called Carlo to serve them similarly. Fr. Robert Gazzaniga,
the chaplain of Carlo's high school, asked him to create
a small online platform to promote volunteer work.
Carlo spent most of the summer of 2006 on it, putting
great effort into mastering Dreamweaver, a program that
computer professionals utilized. During planning meetings, Carlo worked with the chaplain, parents of students,
and the high school's communication team. He did not
lose his composure; he confidently explained his vision
and impressed everyone. The end result was rather good.
He even won a national competition entitled "You will
be a volunteer" (*Sarai volontario*), which seeks to promote
service of various sorts. Carlo's computer skills were recognized by experts in the field, universities, and industry
professionals. In addition to Dreamweaver, he also used
Java, C++, and Ubuntu.

GOD'S COMMUNICATOR

Carlo's objective was to use all his talents for the Church so that young people his age could know and love Jesus like he did. In early August 2002, Carlo, along with his parents, participated in the "Meeting for Friendship between People," which takes place every year in Rimini, on the Adriatic coast. This annual conference, which was organized by the Communion and Liberation movement, brings together different points of view on themes related to culture, religion, politics, and art. These lectures attracted many people in Italy and involved famous leading figures—e.g., former Prime Minister Silvio Berlusconi; Marcello Pera, the former president of the Italian Senate; and the composer Ennio Morricone. The yearly conferences hosted a program of lectures, debates, exhibitions, musical and literary performances, and even athletic events. It was a crossroads for interesting exchanges, and men and women of all ages participated. But in 2002, at the age of eleven, Carlo was clearly among the youngest people there. The theme of that year's conference was "The Sense of Things: The Contemplation of Beauty." Carlo had a taste for beautiful things and lovely landscapes, and he was very interested in the various discussions in which he took part. Some of them were quite philosophical. Most impressive, though, was a series of exhibition panels that presented the historical connections between art and the automobile. Rimini is not far from the Lancia, Ferrari, and Maserati factories, which produce cars that are real objects of art and bear witness to an automotive expertise of which Italians are very proud.

Carlo thought that if cars could be shown this well, why couldn't Christ and the Church be better presented? This is how he got the idea for his exhibition on Eucharistic miracles. His inspiration would take time to mature. How could these miracles best be displayed? How could God's love for the world be communicated today? Carlo worked on this project for two and half years, and he drew his whole family into it. It was a team effort, which he could not have achieved by himself, but which would have never succeeded without Carlo's tenacity.

After more than two years of work, Carlo could not attend the debut of his exhibition, which was launched on October 4, 2006 (the feast of St. Francis of Assisi). The exhibition generated positive reactions for its quality graphics and solid documentation. Cardinal Angelo Comastri wrote the preface to the print edition of this exhibition and concluded exhorting the faithful to "hear the cry of God's love that resonates in each celebration of the Eucharist." On October 4, 2006, Carlo was in the hospital. When his work finally bore fruit, its author was fading. The exhibition was presented in his absence at the Institute of Leo XIII, where he had studied and for which he had already launched a website that included a platform that was devoted to volunteer work. What a coincidence that the launching of his exhibition happened during his illness and his departure from this life! This exhibition, which was developed in an informative and intelligent way and dedicated to his passion, the Eucharist, was his life's masterpiece. Carlo's death would not put an end to the exhibition, however, for it is still continuing his mission today.

Carlo worked hard in gathering information for his exhibition. He was intent on demonstrating that Eucharistic miracles were not legends. They were historical events, that had specific dates and archeological evidence, including reliquaries, marble headstones, and iconographic representations, not to mention scientific tests. Carlo was curious, like many young people his age. But he went all the way with his desire to know. He knew how to capture the attention of those who viewed his exhibition and make them think. Thus, he explained that scientists said that the Lanciano relics were like the fragments of a swollen heart. Carlo knew this was of significance. Receiving the Body and Blood of Jesus was, above all, receiving His Heart, i.e., being in communion with His love. In the Gospel, St. John said, "He loved them to the end" (John 13:1). Carlo knew how to look at ancient mysteries with fresh eyes, in light of God's Word. His exhibition debuted in Rome in a place that bears the name of his patron saint: the Church of San Carlo Borromeo. It's located on the Via del Corso in Rome's historic downtown, an avenue that is the Champs-Élysées of Rome. Similar to the famous street in Paris, people like to stroll past its storefronts on Sunday afternoons to see the latest items showcased. But nothing could top Him who was showcased in Carlo's exhibition.

Since then, his Eucharistic exhibition has traveled to more than 10,000 different places, including churches, schools, congressional palaces, youth clubs, and welcome centers. Carlo is bearing witness in many places he never visited! Similarly, throughout the world and from Carlo's related website, we can still download all of his exhibition panels, which have been translated into eighteen languages, including Russian, Arabic, Singhalese, and Hungarian! In addition, after debuting in Milan, his exhibition traveled to France and then to Belgium. In the United States alone, it has been welcomed into dozens of parishes and more than 100 universities! The bishops of certain countries, like the Philippines, Argentina, and Vietnam, have had it translated into their languages. Some bishops have made commentaries, which have been adapted in China and Indonesia. During the May 2017 canonization of Francisco and Jacinto Marto in Fatima, pilgrims who traveled to Portugal had the added bonus of viewing Carlo's exhibition.

Carlo inspired others to make exhibitions on the Faith. One on angels and demons featured more than 130 related testimonies from saints, including visions and apparitions. Another was on the Mother of God and a third on life after death. In each case, the exhibitions used saints' testimonies, which helped some people rediscover the Faith of the Church, leading them to Christ. In short, Carlo's grand idea still inspires people. There are many themes of our faith that we could try, like him, to present as clearly and simply as he did.

THE RISKS OF THE JOB

But Carlo was not a fool. He knew that in spending hours on his computer, he would be exposed to several risks. He recalled that when he was little, his mother limited the use of video games to one or two hours a week. When he was growing up, the time he spent in front of a screen was primarily devoted to schoolwork. Nonetheless, he had to learn discernment. Before working on the various tasks entrusted to him (such as websites and other evangelization projects), he first had to complete his duties — that is to say, his duties as the son of his parents, as a student in his middle school, and as a Christian. Thus, he always made sure to respect his parents, even if it was sometimes difficult letting go of fully operating scripts when his parents asked him to do something else, such as complete his homework. In spite of his activities, he would always prioritize the daily Mass.

There was also a more serious risk of which he was not too naïve to be ignorant. He was well aware, from the time that he was an adolescent, that the Internet is capable of the worst and the best. There we find real things as well as deceptive lies. Therefore, when we look for information on a Wikipedia page, for example, we must be prudent and always exercise our critical skills. We can find beautiful images on the Internet, like the ones that Carlo used for his set-ups and to illustrate his exhibitions. We also can discover images that destroy the beauty of the soul and body. When Carlo was browsing the Internet, ad blockers and content filters did not exist or were not as easy to use as they are today. He was much more skilled than his parents, who admitted they never knew how to set up parental controls on his computer. Our Carlo was like a lamb in the midst of online wolves, who peddled violent, pornographic, and other problematic content, or who prowled with bad intent on message boards. We cannot underestimate the dangers young people encounter online.

Thus, Carlo had to be prudent. His online history confirms it. Carlo did not have a security code on his computer. He was completely transparent. When he died, his mother discovered the entire extent of his research in his browsing history. She was amazed to see that, despite all these risks, Carlo had not gone astray. This young man has a lot to teach us about using technology as a tool for good instead of evil, and about being more dedicated to real life rather than virtual reality. While spending hours coding, our little geek developed real expertise, and he did not keep his talents to himself. He offered computer courses to those who wanted them, and he provided help to those who were having computer problems because of a technical mishap or virus.

THE CARLO GALAXY

Our little hero was at the heart of a real galaxy, which was more than his own work and the websites he developed. Today, there are almost 1.5 million hits for "Carlo Acutis" in a quick web search, including an official website for his canonization cause,[31] another official site that is for educators, young people, and prayer groups, not to mention the four sites that are dedicated to different exhibitions that he inspired. We can find Carlo in his famous virtual spatial vessel on his website.[32] He coded his interface by imagining himself the pilot of a spacecraft, aboard which he could share his school, friends, favorite animals, in short, his entire daily life, to his passengers. After more than ten years in operation, the graphics are a little out of date. But the platform still functions. We totally believe it when the page opens up, and we hear the *Star Wars* music. The most fun thing about this application that he developed is that he foresaw a whole space for games — from Simon Says to

---

31. http://www.carloacutis.com/es/association.
32. We still find his "spatial vessel" on the official site www.carloacutis.net/space/astronave.html. (As of March 2021, this website is difficult to access because Flash Player has been disabled.)

a replica of Space Invaders or Snake, which he was able to play from his parents' Nokia telephone. This platform shows all of Carlo's playful spirit. If he was holy, he also knew how to have fun. In more than one way, Carlo is, therefore, a true model to show us how to use the Internet well. We can do so many good things with it—e.g., talk about God, but also gain knowledge, have fun, and communicate with others as he did.

The Internet had a hard time finding a patron saint. To be honest, the Church could not find anyone fitting besides an obscure saint of the first millennium named Isidore of Seville. Isidore was born at the end of the sixth century in Andalusia, to the south of today's Spain. His love of studying made him one of the most erudite minds of his time. During that period, Andalusia was a crossroads for people and cultures, meetings and conflicts. In the midst of these crossroads, Isidore wrote an enormous encyclopedia titled *Etymologies*, in which he provides the origins of many different things, ranging from the names of God to agricultural practices. With much knowledge and, at times, a lot of humor, he drew connections between many different subjects. In 2002, the Vatican named Isidore patron of the online world, invoking his intercession to build cultural bridges like the one the saint constructed between antiquity and the Middle Ages. We can also see how Carlo serves as a model for building bridges online, and let us pray that he help us emulate his great example.

PRUDENCE, THE QUEEN OF VIRTUES

"Be well-behaved and be prudent." This is how we often stereotype childhood holiness. But wishing to be a perfect picture, we only end up, as Carlo had said, a photocopy. Carlo did not want any false prudence. He lived with a caution that also knew how to take risks and discern the right time to do the right thing. Prudence is the queen of virtues because, without it, all the other virtues are unbalanced. Strength becomes violent, courage reckless, justice intransigent, and love dissolute. Thanks to prudence, man can conform his actions with right reason. Thus, we can reflect on what we want to do, and try to achieve it as well as possible. What often surprises us about Carlo, and what his teachers could particularly observe, was what a thoughtful young man he was. But his questioning never paralyzed him. We can spend several days discerning our plan of action, but not come up with anything. We then need someone to tell us, "Stop thinking. Do something." Carlo showed us how sincere reflection leads to action. He did not reflect so he could find excuses to do nothing. He thought and, above all, prayed to know how he could, through his actions, participate in doing some good in the world. Was it more important to spend more time with his lonely grandmother or to spend an extra hour working on his exhibition? Was it wiser to go to bed or to spend all night coding? How does one use his computer skills to help others? Prudence, contrary to what we may often think, does not lead to inaction, but rather to action. It is on this condition that man's prudence can participate in God's Providence. God created a world full of intelligence, in which we observe the physical laws of nature and also discern and apply the natural moral law, which is in accord with our divinely created human nature. God always acts prudently. When we use our God-given reason and thereby also act prudently, we can participate well in His divine Providence.

THE WORD OF GOD

Behold, I send you out as sheep in the midst of wolves; so be wise as serpents and innocent as doves. (Matt. 10:16)

LIFE QUESTIONS

➢ How much time do I spend in front of a screen?

➢ Have I become addicted?

➢ How can I use the Internet to deepen my faith?

➢ How do I ask God to guide my actions?

➢ Do my presence on the Internet and my attitude on social networks bear witness to God's love?

PRAYER TO GOD

God of my fathers and Lord of mercy, You created the universe through Your Word. You formed man, through Your wisdom, to be the master of Your creatures, to govern the world with justice and holiness, and thus to render righteous judgments.

Give me the wisdom that sits by Your throne. Do not cut me off from Your many children. I am Your servant, the son of Your servant, and a frail man who does not last long. I am too weak to understand Your precepts and laws. If the most accomplished of the children of men lacks the wisdom that You offer, he will not count for anything. Give me the wisdom that sits by Your throne.

Chapter 6
The Teenager in Love (with God)

CRISIS HOTLINE

 When he was an adolescent, Carlo spent hours on the phone with his friends. Whether he was sitting on the sofa in the living room or walking about, gesturing with his free hand.

Sometimes, talking on the telephone is simpler. It acts as a filter and we more easily confide in each other. So, Carlo found himself listening for hours to his friends' confidences at the end of the line. The following scene often occurred in the Acutis home. The home phone would ring. Nobody picked up. The ringing continued. Finally, Mrs. Acutis answered, "Hello?—Yes, hello, may I speak to Carlo, please?—Who is it?—Ambra, a middle school friend." Then, his mother would put the phone down and call to her son, "Carlo, it's for you again!" Carlo would burst into view and start a conversation that could last hours. His friends shared their problems, seeking advice.

His mother often asked him: "Don't you see each other enough in school? Do you still have to talk to each other for the whole night?"

Social networks have increased the intensity of communication between teens, for better or for worse. For if young people can trust each other, they can also betray each other. The public disclosure of shared secrets creates deep wounds and humiliation. One thing is certain: Carlo knew how to listen and keep things confidential, which is why his friends trusted him. He also knew how to counsel and sometimes correct his friends when they wandered into dead-end relationships. They called to share their disappointments with him and also, at times, the grievances they held against others. Carlo's phone became a crisis hotline for reconciling friends arguing among themselves. Often these arguments were triggered for ridiculous reasons. Yet, Carlo never tired of listening. Consequently, we might think Carlo could have made a good priest confessor had he lived long enough. While his goal was clearly holiness, he did not scorn the sometimes superficial or imperfect lives of his friends. He knew how to listen without criticism and kindly respond to them. For him, it was about offering everyone the love that was his.

FROM CRAZY LOVE TO FALSE LOVE

Because he was such a good friend, others liked to share their secrets with Carlo, especially their first loves. When we "fall in love," we can lead with our hearts and not with our heads, and therefore discover our hearts' fragility. A budding love is like a small flame that must be protected, in the hope of it someday being transformed into a beautiful blaze. Many teens more easily confide in their friends than in their parents. Often, we do not dare speak to our parents about our first love. Obviously, when our parents see our faces, they suspect something. But we prefer to confide in our friends — sometimes due to shame or discomfort. When he fell in love with Juliet, Romeo confided in Mercutio. When Carlo's friends wanted to share about their love, they often called Carlo. Mercutio's advice was frequently full of rancor. Carlo's heart was not rancorous, but jealous. His jealousy was the sort of jealously we refer to when we say that God is jealous. God is jealous of His people when they deviate and wallow in debauchery and idolatry, such as when the Israelites betrayed their covenant with the Lord: "They stirred him to jealousy" (Deut. 32:16). God so loved His people that He wanted them to experience the happiness of an exclusive and faithful covenant. In the same way, Carlo could sometimes be jealous. He was eager for the love of God and the love of the world. He was jealous when he saw his female friends lose themselves in the arms of boys who were only tearing them down.

Compared with our grandparents' generation, today's girls and boys more easily confide openly to each other about their lives. But love has been so trivialized through the thousands of images bombarded on us by the media that we no longer know what should be appreciated in secret: we kiss without shame, we make love in a mechanical way, transforming what is most intimate about the relationship between a man and woman into coffee shop conversation. Carlo knew it was difficult to talk about sexuality without being crude or vulgar. At the same time, he refused to be holier-than-thou by sticking to prudish answers.

One time a female friend revealed her feelings for a boy with whom she had become passionately involved. She told Carlo everything, including her "first time." What could Carlo say? Why did she put him in that position? Was she feeling proud or guilty? If Carlo said nothing, he would be merely a voyeur interested in love stories not his own. But if he responded, what could his answer be? Finally, how to explain why not? As long as they love each other! But infatuation so quickly becomes false love. When his fourteen-year-old friend told him of her first time, he felt hurt, first of all. She, like him, was baptized and received Communion on Sundays. So, why would she let herself be drawn into infidelity? How could she commune both with this boy's body, which she would forget after a few evenings, and with the Body of Christ, who brought her into a communion with God for all eternity?

In the depth of his being, Carlo knew that we all want to be loved and appreciated, but that sometimes we can let ourselves be tempted by loves that disappoint us. Carlo would often repeat this sentence: "Remember that your body is the Temple where God's Spirit wants to dwell." He was saddened to see that we forget this dignity for superficial pleasures. One day, a female friend, who had gone to a nightclub, told him: "It's okay. Stop being a daddy!" She was fourteen. It was not choirboys or even boys of her own age that she encountered there. Carlo said to this friend: "Try to respect yourself. If you can't do this, at least respect Love." Carlo was not naïve and did not need a biology courses to tell him that we cannot make love the way we make a cake. Our bodies are meaningful, and their gestures speak to us. There is a love language that is not written, but that our bodies express. As we can sometimes lie with words, we can also betray love with our bodies. Thus, some of the most beautiful gestures become a sham when we divorce them from their meaning. When we are in church and, during the sign of peace, shake hands with a hypocritical smile, not looking into each other's eyes in reconciliation, we betray and flout the peace that Christ came to give us. We empty the gesture He invites us to make. The same thing is true for our bodies.

Carlo was obviously aware that relationships between teenagers are subject to a lot of pressure to the point of not always being consenting. They often go further than either of them would want. Carlo's friends let themselves be swept away by what the crowd did. They did not resist because, after all, everyone was doing the same thing. Carlo was a resistance fighter for love and a rebel for authentic love—a love that does not need to protect itself and play at something that it cannot yet be. There is a certain irony in the mouth of his female friend who told him not "to be a daddy," for he was not the one who was acting like a daddy or mommy. On the contrary, all that Carlo wanted was to be able to love as a teenager can love and to let himself calmly grow in freedom.

GIRLFRIENDS

Did Carlo have a girlfriend? With his pure heart, we could have the false impression that he preferred living in an ivory tower. Even if he seemed naïve, girls of his age were not indifferent to him. He caught the eye of more than one of them. Carlo was cheerful and kind. He knew how to be of service and listen. In a nutshell, Carlo was the perfect boyfriend. Carlo was not stingy with friends. He maintained true and sincere friendships with girls his age. Yet, he was nothing more than a friend. Friendship starts with respect. If many people today don't think boys and girls can be real friends, it is because there is no more respect. It is a respect whose modesty, gallantry, and elegance were hallmarks for our grandparents. Even some Christians doubt such friendship is possible. Yet, all you have to do is turn to Jesus, who loved to spend time with Martha and

Mary in Bethany. He even made Mary Magdalene the first witness of His Resurrection. Are we ready to believe in this kind of friendship—the one between St. Benedict and St. Scholastica or between St. Francis and St. Claire of Assisi? Carlo believed in such friendship, and his young female friends bore witness to it. But his friendship did not stop at the Facebook friendships we have today. It was an incarnate friendship. The purity of his intentions was demonstrated by his fidelity. Carlo didn't chase after girls. He developed privileged connections with them. When one of his female friends was sad, Carlo didn't hesitate to give her a consoling hug. Carlo believed in love, and he did not want to play at being in love. He knew that going further would not benefit a female friend going through hardship but would only be self-serving.

He was even worried about the superficial relationships that many boys of his own age sought to have with girls. These saddened him. He saw that young people were, in part, victims of the society in which they lived, a society that continually bombarded them with distorted messages about the relationship between men and women. Carlo knew, for example, that pornography is a terrible distortion of the truth. It is an industry that reduces the woman to an animal state, and the man to his animal desire. It turns women into object s of gratification and subjection and leads the viewer to believe that his desire merges with reality. Through the strength of its images and the incredible degree of violence, it destroys childhood innocence without notice and nourishes nauseating fantasies that grow more perverted and misdirected. Carlo observed the consequences of this degradation of the woman's image. When boys his age hit on his female friends at the pool, he did not hesitate to put them back in their place. It angered him to see boys whistle at girls the same way that people whistle at dogs. Carlo had come to swim and not to see his female friends be harassed. One of his friends replied: "It's okay, Carlo. We have a right to have fun!" "Excuse me, but I'm not enjoying it. We're not brutes. God created a body for us to be the temple of the Spirit. We must respect the body—other people's bodies and ours as well." His intransigence did not please everyone. But it earned him a lot of respect from his female friends. It was an issue of justice for him.

A LOVER OF HUMAN LIFE FROM ITS CONCEPTION

Carlo was a lover of life. When he was around fourteen years old, his natural curiosity led him to make further progress in his love for it. His spontaneous love for life would become a rational love to defend those that are weakest. He would draw from this awareness as part of a school assignment. During a cellular biology class, his natural science teacher assigned a report on bioethics. The idea was to connect their course on the functioning of cells with other subjects like

philosophy, law, or religion. Carlo came across a complicated subject that he knew nothing about a priori—stem
cells and Judaism. Starting in the '90s, stem cells, which
are developed from the moment of conception, were the
object of much research. Many debates about human embryonic stem cells have had to do with issues dealing with
restrictions applied to studies that use these types of cells
if they do not respect the value of each life. But when do
we know when life starts? Such was not an easy topic for a
young teenager to deal with. After much online research,
he presented his report. He explained to his friends that in
the Jewish religion, the embryo is thought to be a person
only from the fortieth day of its development, which is the
day when nerve cells grow. It was, therefore, acceptable for
some scientific Jews to create embryos in order to produce
stem cells from a therapeutic perspective. But the Jewish
community was not unanimous on this issue. Some feared
shifts toward unnatural experiments such as those conducted
in countries like China, where some laboratories claimed
to create hybrid human-animal embryos or clones, without,
to this day, any evidence of success. The Church asserts,
in accordance with modern embryology, that the embryo
is a living, complete, integrated, and autonomous being
that, if gifted with a favorable environment, moves along a
path of development until maturation. Because of this position, the Catholic Church is opposed to research on human
embryonic stem cells, which requires the destruction of the

human embryo during its harvesting. On the other hand, the Church has defended research on adult stem cells, which do not call for human embryonic stem cells. Moreover, it highlights the scientific progress in this field, which has led to the development of ethical codes[33] for research as well as preferred medical treatments. It is not surprising that such a technical and fascinating subject interested Carlo. As a student, he realized that, behind the complicated words were fragile lives. He grew more aware of the extent to which life could be loved, from the first moment of conception. This was about growing in the admiration of the mystery of life and respecting the dignity of each living being. It was, again, a question of justice.

FRANCIS' ROSES

Finally, when looking at Carlo's life, we can be tempted to think that everything was easy for him. We believe that he was holy because he died young and did not have time to be tempted by the world's pleasures. Those who are currently fifteen years old, or can remember when they were fifteen, know better. Others prefer to see Carlo as an angel, rather than a human teenager. He was so innocent. Who could have questioned the purity of his heart? Sometimes, we

---

33. The recent breakthrough in the reprogramming of somatic cells into induced pluripotent cells (iPSCs) of an embryonic type has, in fact, once more reduced the argument in favor of the use of embryonic stem cells.

might say the same thing about Mary. She was without sin. So how could she have been tempted? We forget what Scripture teaches us, starting with the book of Genesis. The first man was both holy and sinless when he was tempted. Indeed, Adam had never transgressed before dragging down all of humanity into his downfall. Therefore, the more we grow in holiness, the holier we are, the more serious the consequences of sin are and the more they deform us. The higher up we go, the lower we can fall. The struggle for purity is intensified as we grow in holiness. We see it in the lives of the great saints, through the strong manifestations of demonic temptations in the life of a Curé of Ars or a Padre Pio. This same was true for Carlo, especially since he was like us. Carlo had nothing to hide from us. Like us, he was confronted with the challenges of puberty and adolescence. And if he did not fall, nothing prevents us from thinking that he was not tempted. How was he able to resist? How could he keep smiling while the difficult transitions toward adulthood often provoke a certain bitterness in the teenager? How was he able to preserve the purity of his childhood while gaining maturity? The confessional secret that endures after death and the absence of a diary prevent us from answering these questions. But there is a place that Carlo loved that give a us a hint.

His parents enjoyed taking Carlo on trips during their vacations. This is how he visited so many countries in his short life. But as the years went by, Carlo no longer dreamed of going far away — to corners of the world more exotic. Instead, as he grew older, Carlo wished to spend more and more time in Umbria, a region in central Italy between Rome and Milan. Assisi became his favorite place, so much so that his parents bought a second home there. The whole world knows about this city, thanks to a certain poor little man — *il poverello* — named Francis Bernardone, who became the founder of a religious community that continues to impact the world more than 800 years later. Like Carlo, Francis was born to an influential merchant father. As a young man growing up in a commercial town in the Middle Ages, Francis chose to strip himself of everything — even his clothes — so that he could live in poverty, like Christ. Carlo felt happy in this picturesque town under the shadow of Mount Subasio. He often went for walks with his parents and dogs on the nearby hiking trails.

Carlo also made two friends in Assisi, Mattia and Jacopo, with whom he enjoyed playing soccer. He often played soccer with his friends, whether on vacation or after school in Milan. Carlo was a fan of AC Milan, a professional soccer team, and while he surely followed the FIFA World Cups, he was not a soccer nut either. From time to time, though, Carlo did like playing five-on-five games with his friends in Milan. Meanwhile, when not playing soccer in Assisi, Carlo went back to his room, which was on the mezzanine level of the home his parents had purchased in the old city. We can still imagine him retreating to his room, as if climbing to a personal tree house. From that room, far from the hustle and bustle of the city, he could dream, pray, read, or he would walk the winding streets and up and down Assisi's maze of stairways.

Carlo loved Assisi. He found a big brother there, for that is where a beautiful friendship with St. Francis, his role model, began. He liked simplicity and a spontaneous way of praying. He enjoyed singing to God along with Francis, praising Him for everything that He created. Francis was so angelic that he was called the "seraph." But Francis was also tried and tested. They say that once, when he had already taken up the cowl and adopted a life of poverty, he was still tempted by the charming women of Assisi. Rather than throwing himself in their arms, he preferred to throw himself into a thorny bed of roses. Through a miracle, the thorns of this rosebush fell off. We can still see this rosebush without thorns in Assisi, which reminds us of this story. Beyond its legendary character, this anecdote has something to teach us about the way St. Francis experienced temptation. Rather than yield, he preferred to accept his suffering. God transformed the pain of those thorns into a rose of tenderness. Carlo did not tell us about the details of his trials. But, for a long time, he poured his heart out to God in prayer and adoration and entrusted all his joys and struggles to the Lord. If he found a model to follow Christ in St. Francis, we can imagine that he also saw a model to resist temptations in him. This was a model through which he learned to die to himself while continuing to smile and subject his pride toward the love of his neighbor.

A MOTHER WHO WAS TRANSFORMED BY THE LOVE OF HER SON

Finally, the best source to learn about Carlo's love is undoubtedly the one who loved him since he was conceived. Who knows a child the best? It is his mother. Carlo's mother is the one who talks about him most naturally and simply today. Incidentally, when God wants to use an image to express how much He cares for His people, He uses the metaphor of a mother in the Bible: "Before I formed you in the womb I knew you" (Jer. 1:5.) His mother loved him with this kind of love. But if she was the first one to love Carlo, he was the first one to teach her to love Heaven. Carlo became a teacher in the Faith for his mother. She had grown up in a rather ordinary secular family, yet she let herself be challenged by all of the questions her son had for her. She testified: "Having a son who so insistently asked me questions about the Faith made me think. This was a reason for me to approach the Church and the sacraments."

She very affectionately calls Carlo her "little savior," the one who let her take this special path. This is a path on which she continues, including by sharing widely her son's witness, especially his exhibition on Eucharistic miracles, which has already traveled to five continents and helped so many people understand the greatness of God's love. She wants the world to know about Carlo's love, trust, and hope, a beautiful testimony he left in the last words that he spoke to her: "Mom, don't be afraid. Since Jesus became a man, death has become the passage toward life, and we don't need to flee it. Let us prepare ourselves to experience something extraordinary in the eternal life."

LOVE AND JUSTICE

When we speak about love to young people as educators, we typically emphasize prudence and temperance, often forgetting about justice in the process. We need to avoid two extremes: On the one hand, we can't impose rigid rules to control everything. On the other, we can't be merely indifferent or even complicit in young people's transgressions, saying, "Do what you want to do. It's not serious. You will make more important choices when you're grown up"—as if teenagers' choices are only superficial problems that do not affect their hearts and bodies. They make right and important choices now. They will not know how to love well when they are forty-five years old if teens do not learn how from the time they are fifteen. Society often pressures young people to be content with a superficial morality.

Social networks encourage an excessive visual culture. We try to *look* more than just *be*. Parents, who did not have these tools in their childhood, do not necessarily know how to use them. They are sometimes the first ones to get caught in their traps; whereas parental controls allow for a more responsible use of the networks for children. There is a tendency on networks, which are hidden behind marketing campaigns, to separate beauty from truth. Online influencers become empty shells and the idols for impressionable young people. They are only looking to win followers, even if it means lying about what they do and who they are, while hiding behind their online filters. What do we do to warn young people about the risks of these social networks?

In order to avoid bad influences, some parents strive to awaken their children's awareness of their responsibilities: "Accept the consequence of your actions." This is good, but it's not enough. Others have stricter prohibitions. "Don't do this. Don't do that." In both cases, this deals only with an external morality. Love is not simply an issue of prudence or temperance, but also of justice. It is not merely about imposing and observing external rules, but about developing a more interior rule of life — a sense of justice. Justice is the virtue that gives everyone what he deserves. We may tell ourselves that justice has nothing to do with love. Doesn't love have the right to love who it wants as it wants? Making rules in this field is complicated. We quickly switch between laxity and rigidity. How far can we go? At what age can we start being interested in love? The prevailing culture tells us that there is no answer to these questions and that everyone answers them in his own way.

Yet, after years of promoting uninhibited enjoyment and love without justice, the West is waking up with a hangover and shattered lives. Love without justice can ruin lives—the lives of bullied women, abused children, and young porn addicts. This is a generation unjustly deprived of knowing real love. It is time to give justice to all these denied loves. Carlo was a vigilante for love who wanted to give everyone the love that he deserved. However, he was not a moral dictator. He knew that there was no justice without freedom, and that everyone must make a free commitment to love. He knew that giving everyone the love he or she deserved was not imposing a straitjacket but restoring a sense of his dignity to everyone. This choice of love is recognizing that everyone is unique in God's eyes. God loves each one of us personally and in varied ways. God is not unjust because everyone is unique. It is up to us to give everyone—God, our parents, and friends, as well as ourselves—the love that they deserve.

THE WORD OF GOD

This is my commandment, that you love one another as I have loved you. Greater love has no man than this, that a man lay down his life for his friends. (John 15:12–13)

LIFE QUESTIONS

➢ Have I said "I love You!" to God?

➢ Who is the person on the earth whom I love the most?

➢ Are some of my loves and even my self-love sometimes out of order? How can I adjust them?

➢ How should I react when I see my friends involved in toxic relationships?

➢ What is my self-image, and what is my relationship to visual images in general?

PRAYER TO GOD

I love You, O my God, and my sole desire is to love You until the last breath of my life.

I love You, O infinitely lovable God, and I prefer to die loving You than to live one instant without loving You.

I love You, O my God, and I do not desire anything but Heaven so as to have the joy of loving You perfectly.

I love You, O my God, and I fear Hell, because there will not be the sweet consolation of loving You.

O my God, if my tongue cannot say in every moment that I love You, I want my heart to say it in every beat. Allow me the grace to suffer loving You, to love You suffering, and one day to die loving You and feeling that I love You. And as I approach my end, I beg You to increase and perfect my love of You.

Amen.

"Act of Love," St. John Vianney (the Curé of Ars)

Chapter 7
At Heaven's Gates

HIS LAST TRIP

Carlo said that "God has written a unique and unrepeatable story for each of us. But He gave every one of us the freedom to choose the end." Our last chapter, relating Carlo's last trip, took place in 2006. Yet the end arrives too quickly in all good stories. On May 27, 2006, at 5:54 a.m. local time, an unusually violent earthquake—6.2 on the Richter scale—devastated the Indonesian island of Java. It caused 5,782 deaths and 36,299 casualties; 105,000 homes were destroyed; 650,000 people were on the streets. Why did the earth convulse? Why did nature take control over the lives of men, women, and children who could do nothing to escape it? How can God allow innocent people to die? Such tragic events provoke waves of emotions. Very often, a surge of generosity then brings the international community together to come to the aid of the disaster victims. But today, who still recalls this earthquake? We have the same feeling of disarray when facing armed conflicts. These continue to wipe out entire populations in the world without anyone's remembering the lesson of the horror of war that is on constant repeat. So many events briefly fill our screens before being replaced by another image. Sometimes, we are saturated with news to such an extent that other events, which are, nonetheless, sad and serious, seem inconsequential. That year, another innocent person left us. Nobody expected it. Time was running out for Carlo, who reached the heavenly homeland on October 12, 2006. Carlo returned to His Father.

THE END TIMES

Death is not usually a subject that fifteen-year-old teenagers take on. Yet, on his spiritual journey, Carlo always kept in mind what we traditionally call "The Four Last Things"—death, judgment, Heaven, and Hell. When he talked about death, it was not with fear or contempt, but with the strength of faith that provides hope. However, he did not produce any films about Heaven by trying, at all costs, to know what it looked like. He knew that Heaven was being with Jesus, and that was enough for him. There is a famous song in France by the artist Michel Polnareff: "We Will All Go to Heaven." But Carlo thought that, without Jesus, we do not go anywhere. He knew it was impossible to go directly to Heaven by our own strength. He wrote notes to those who did not believe in the afterlife, and explained Heaven, Hell, and Purgatory at his own level. The questions for him was not, "Is Heaven real?" but "How do you go there?" The question of salvation was important for Carlo in his relationship with others. He never lost sight of it. Carlo really wanted everyone to go to Heaven. In his scattered notes, we understand how important it is to strive for eternity from the time you start living on earth. He believed that if eternity was life in the Spirit, we could start to cooperate here on earth in the work of the Spirit. By living in conformity with the Gospel, Carlo knew we can experience on earth a foretaste of Heaven. His father wrote, Carlo's relationship with the Lord helped him be ready for death: "My son experienced an absolutely normal life. But he always kept in mind that, sooner or later, we all had to die. When I asked Him: 'What will you do when you grow up?' he replied: 'Only God knows the future.'"

Andrea Acutis excelled at selling the best life insurance in Italy. But he found the assurance of life eternal, thanks to his son: it was a complete trust in the Resurrection of Christ. But not everyone had his faith. Many of his close friends' thoughts on what happened after death were a bit of an impressionistic blur. Nothing was certain. They thought the most likely end for them was decomposition and disappearance. The doubts of his close friends, which Carlo sometimes shared, encouraged him to do more research and deepen his faith. He left enough notes to allow his postulator, Nicola Gori, to complete a new exhibition on the end times entitled, "Hell, Purgatory, and Heaven." Starting with the witness of the saints — of those who had visions of Heaven and Hell — this exhibition provides pedagogical insight on life after death in light of Scripture and the Church's teaching. The children in Fatima were not hallucinating when they saw Hell, and Jesus was not lying when, on the Cross, He said to the good thief: "And he said to him, "Truly, I say to you, today you will be with me in Paradise" (Luke 23:43).

A FATAL DIAGNOSIS

Sometimes, life changes. A beautiful autumn day shifts, in a few moments, from a summer sun to a thick fog. Carlo had never had any serious illnesses or heavy medical treatment. Less than two weeks before his death, he was very much alive. He had been working on the last details for the opening of his exhibition on Eucharistic miracles, which he had been anticipating for two years. Finally, the big day arrived. In the excitement of the preparations, he had completely given of himself and now he felt somewhat tired. Around October 1, 2006, he started to feel an inflammation in the area of his throat. His parents brought him to their attending physician. There was, apparently, nothing to worry about. It was a simple parotitis, which a doctor friend confirmed. Carlo only had an inflammation of his salivary glands, which may have been the result of dehydration. But the inflammation continued and, a few days later, his symptoms worsened. The pain was terrible, and Carlo's urine suddenly became red. He had hematuria, that is to say, his blood was mixing with his urine. His parents immediately had laboratory analyses done. When they asked him if he was doing well, Carlo replied: "Dad, Mom, I am offering all these sufferings for the Pope and the Church." Carlo was clearly suffering, but he did not want to complain. Bearing this without flinching was heroic. The laboratory analyses did not detect anything abnormal.

But things did not improve. On Sunday morning, October 8, whereas he usually woke up with a lot of energy to go to Sunday Mass, he was completely weak. We could consign this exhaustion to his work on the completion of his exhibition. But this was much more than simple overworking. His body was completely depleted. He was so tired that he could not even get out of bed. His parents called the pediatrician who had been monitoring him since he was a child. This doctor worked in a clinic that specialized in children's blood diseases. He immediately understood that the situation was serious. Carlo was transported to the clinic, and its medical team had the grim responsibility of announcing the diagnosis to Mr. and Mrs. Acutis. Carlo was afflicted with leukemia, a cancer of the blood. In

addition, he had one of the worst types—acute promyelocytic leukemia. How would the doctors explain to Carlo's
parents that their only son had almost no chance of recov-
ering from his sickness? How would they tell this young
teenager, who had his whole life in front of him, that he
would now be facing imminent death? Yet, the law that was
in effect required the doctor to tell him the truth.

Promyelocytic leukemia is an acute myeloblastic
leukemia. It begins in abnormal myeloid stem cells. Myeloid
stem cells normally change into red or white blood cells
or platelets. This transformation does not correctly occur
in the case of promyelocytic leukemia.[34] In a nutshell, the
bone marrow no longer supplies the body with the blood
it needs in order to live. This leukemia was spreading so
rapidly that any medical treatment had little hope of helping
Carlo. The symptoms were simple onsets of bruises, a hemor-
rhagic diathesis,[35] and a fatigue, which were immediately
present in Carlo. He was, therefore, terminally ill. The
doctors did everything they could to reduce his pain, but it
was acute. After receiving his diagnosis, Carlo took a deep
breath and exclaimed to his parents, "The Lord wanted to
wake me up!"

---

34. In this type of leukemia, a translocation occurs between chromosomes
15 and 17. It causes an interruption of the differentiation of the white blood
cells that are produced in the bone marrow, and which are present in the
blood at the promyelocytic stage, before their differentiation.
35. A blood clotting disorder that causes a series of hemorrhages.

Carlo was subsequently rushed to the intensive care unit, where he received a respirator mask because his breathing had become more and more difficult. The mask helped him to inhale, but it prevented Carlo from exhaling normally and even coughing, which increased his pain. He blurted out this sentence to his parents, which said a lot about the fierceness of the suffering he was bearing: "Dad, Mom, I am already experiencing my Purgatory, and I want to go straight to Heaven." Only his mother was authorized to stay with him until dusk. Then the doctors asked her to leave. Carlo was unable to sleep. He stayed by himself, with his machines—like Jesus, who was alone in His agony in the Mount of Olives and like so many sick people who face illness alone. He did not sleep a wink until the early morning. His mother and grandmother stayed in the rooms that were provided for the family in case the situation suddenly became worse.

In the morning, they came first thing to Carlo's bedside. At the request of the department head, Carlo was then transported by ambulance to San Gerardo Hospital in Monza, a specialist hospital a little north of Milan. This hospital had a specialized center for Carlo's leukemia diagnosis. Only three hospitals in Italy were equipped with such a center to treat this rare illness. Beds were provided in this hospital to let his mother and grandmother spend the night in the same room with him. This gave them much relief.

A WITNESS FOR CHRIST UP UNTIL HIS LAST BREATH

Without delay, Mrs. Acutis called for the hospital chaplain. Carlo received the Sacrament of the Anointing of the Sick. When the nurse asked him how he was feeling, he replied, "I'm okay. I'm doing well." Knowing the seriousness of his illness and the suffering that it implied better than Carlo did, the nurse insisted, "Are you sure that you're doing well?" Carlo responded, "There are some for whom it's worse." Carlo's life was hanging by the proverbial thread, and that thread would soon be broken. The entire medical team that accompanied him in these key hours were struck by his detachment and perseverance up until the end. In his beatification file, his nurse testified:

I only had a few hours to get to know Carlo. But these are moments that will always remain in my mind. Despite his illness, there was a sparkle of life in his eyes, and he did everything to crack a smile to anyone who was talking to him. When he was not able to answer the doctors' questions, he asked for forgiveness as if he had done something wrong. That is real humility. In the evening, he asked me, above all, not to wake up his parents. "You know, they are already so tired." He did not, in particular, want to worry them more. When I took his hand to try to reassure him, he was the one who gave me more peace and serenity.

That night was terrible. While the nurse tried to tell him that it was not the end, Carlo told him that it was really over: "I have to leave." The nurse did not want to believe it. He spent the time holding his hand and encouraging him: "I wanted, at all costs, to see him again the next day and to stay with him on the following night. But finally, he knew better than I did."

A little before sunrise, Carlo, who had not slept for hours, fell into a coma. The life support monitors were all blinking red. Once again doctors rushed Carlo to the intensive care unit on a stretcher. In another attempt to save his life, Carlo underwent a special cleansing of all his blood, which separated the red and white blood cells. The operation was successful. But just as a vague hope started to reappear, Carlo suffered a cerebral hemorrhage. The flow of blood was indisputable. The situation was fatal. On October 11, 2006, the doctor pronounced Carlo brain dead.

The question of an organ donation came up, but Carlo's blood had contaminated all of his organs. No organ dona-tion was possible. As is often the case during a child's death, his heart continued to beat. His heart stopped beating at 6:45 a.m. on October 12, 2006.

REFLECTING THE PIETA

His parents gave him life, and life gave them a dead child. The injustice made Antonia and Andrea sob and weep. They could expect everything except the loss of their only child. Does a father deserve this? How do you console a mother who has lost her child? How does one understand what is happening? It is said the Virgin Mary's heart was pierced by her Son's pain at the foot of the Cross. She received His dead body in her arms—she who had given Him life. We can only imagine the sense of abandonment of Carlo's parents, who were deprived of their life's treasure. Yet, this black cloud already had its silver lining. Carlo's parents testify today that a light of hope shone in their hearts amid their sadness, despite their inability to understand death's separation. Their solitude soon turned into a multitude. After the mortuary cleansed Carlo's body, his parents were given special permission to bring their son's body home to watch over it until the funeral. His high school friends, who had been waiting for the unveiling of his exhibition almost as impatiently as he was, had been informed about Carlo's condition as soon as his health had declined. When they learned of his death, the news spread as instant as a text message throughout the city. His friends crowded at the front of the door to ring the Acutis family's doorbell, so as to pray near their friend Carlo, who had died in the odor of sanctity. For four days, an uninterrupted procession of friends, loved ones, and strangers came to pray, shed tears, and console Carlo's parents.

Four days later, on October 15, the news had spread throughout all of Milan. People were torn between disbelief and sadness. Was it really young Carlo the news was about? But how was this possible? And why him? He had seemed to be in such good health, did so much good, and was undoubtedly one of the most remarkable young persons in school. Why did he have to go first? Everyone in the parish was talking about it. Carlo's parents saw an immense crowd of strangers come to his funeral. This included his friends, of course, but also those whose relationship with Carlo they were unaware. There were the building caretakers whom he greeted, classroom teachers with whom he talked, and friends from school. Above all, to his parents' surprise, came many simple people far from the upscale social environment Antonia and Andrea inhabited. Carlo had touched a lot of people in his short life. His funeral did not have the usual seriousness one associates with burial. Those who came to say goodbye one more time were indescribably joyful. How was that possible? They should have been sad, and yet, for the most part, they were joyful. Joy flowed in the tears, and the faces of all the faithful were full of hope. The priest gave the final blessing at noon. Usually, at the end of funerals, church bells soberly sound the death knell. But in this case, as on every Thursday at noon, the people heard the ringing of the Angelus bells. The Angelus is the prayer of Christians who, three times a day, recall the Good News that the Angel Gabriel announced to Mary. The bells were ringing as if to proclaim that, if Carlo had died on earth, he had just been born in Heaven.

HOW A DEVOTION WAS BORN

The expressions of support and signs of affection converged from everywhere. Two people later testified about the exceptional favors they received at Carlo's funeral Mass.[36] Many young people of fifteen, who had decided to no longer spend time at church, returned for his funeral. And because of the joy they experienced, they came back for the third month's Mass. The crowd kept growing. An association, "Friends of Carlo Acutis," even had to be formalized to organize the Requiem Masses that were annually offered on Carlo's behalf. Each time, people stayed longer to tell each other about an anecdote or memory of this young man, who had left a mark on their lives. One day, while she was in Rome, Carlo's mother met with the editor of *L'Osservatore*

---

36. A woman testified about the disappearance of a cancerous tumor. In addition, a married couple, who had struggled with infertility for several years, connected the birth of their child nine months later to Carlo's funeral Mass, in which the child's mother had participated. The canonization process seeks to evaluate such remarkable events, particularly miracles, that occur after a deceased holy person — in this case, Carlo — is asked to intercede with God for answers to prayer.

Romano.[37] He was a close family friend who had talked to Carlo during a family visit to Saint Peter's Basilica. The editor advised Carlo's mother to have an official biography written about her son. Such a book would help ensure an objective account of Carlo's life by collecting testimonies and gathering the documents Carlo left behind him. These included childhood photos, letters, personal notes and, of course, the preliminary documents for his exhibition on the Eucharist. This objective work had to be accomplished so that the truth of Carlo's life would not be lost in pious legend. Real investigative work was needed, for even Carlo's parents knew they did not have the complete version of his life. The newspaper's editor thus offered to entrust the investigation to one of his journalists, Nicola Gori, who was fascinated by the life of this little genius. When he was done with his research, he published a biography entitled *The Eucharist: My Highway to Heaven* (*Eucaristia: La Mia Autostrada per il Cielo*).[38]

The publication of this biography only increased interest in Carlo shown by crowds of strangers. Moreover, his mother strove, with the association of the "Friends," to make Carlo's spiritual heritage known by rotating his exhibition on the Eucharistic miracles, which tours Catholic parishes and universities in Italy and Europe. When a devotion grows so

---

37. *L'Osservatore Romano* is the Vatican's semi-official daily newspaper.
38. Edizioni San Paolo.

quickly and to such an extent, Church leaders take notice. On October 12, 2012, on the sixth anniversary of his departure to Heaven, the Archdiocese of Milan opened the cause for canonization for the one who many believed was a hero of the faith.

But questions must be asked. Before encouraging a devotion, the Church must investigate to see if there are no objections. Did the object of this devotion truly deserve it? Was the life of the one who is being honored truly worthy of this honor? Are his teachings unorthodox, deviant, or deceptive, or do they help transmit the Faith and teaching of the Magisterium? Is this a cult of personality, or does it make those who follow grow in the love of Christ and the life of the Church? We must be assured that Carlo was not "an idol for young people," but rather, a model and source of inspiration, not only for young people, but for today's Christians. On May 13, 2013, on the anniversary of Our Lady's apparitions in Fatima, the Congregation for the Causes of Saints gave its first go-ahead. *Nihil obstat.* Nothing stands in the way of our seeing a new model for living a holy life today in Carlo.

A NEW WAY OF BECOMING HOLY

Everything was getting off to a good start in Carlo's beatification process. Yet, an unexpected problem quickly showed up. To be canonized, you usually have to have had an extraordinary life that is different from the life of us average mortals and lead a life closer to the life of average saints. Can the same really be said of Carlo? Finally, is living a rather exemplary childhood so extraordinary? Can we not say the same thing about many other children? Nobody has ever said otherwise, but was Carlo too normal to be recognized as a saint? He had performed no great miracles, didn't go on any distant mission, nor establish a religious order or congregation. What can arouse such an interest in the virtue of this young man, who was a little too much like us? Clearly, people have become enthusiastic about the holiness of his adolescence. Everyone is well aware that in today's world, with all its challenges and temptations that did not exist a few years earlier, holiness in adolescence has something heroic about it. By looking at Carlo Acutis' file, the Church is not trying to promote a new idea. But it is listening to the instinct of the world's faithful, who see in a young fifteen-year-old man the model the world needs today; who shows us that it's still possible to be holy. A saint who is normal and like us is extraordinary.

Pope Francis admires this type holiness so much that he is even speaking of a new way of becoming holy.[39] In the early days of Christianity, it was common to think that, in order to be holy, it was better to die as a martyr. Thus, there are few known saints in the first millennium who did not

---

39. Pope Francis, *Motu proprio Maiorem hac dilectionem*, July 11, 2017.

die to bear witness to the Faith, offering this final witness of their love for God and their brothers. When the persecutions in the Roman Empire had ceased, the question of how to continue to offer one's life for God was asked. It was at this time that a young Roman man, the future St. Alexis, who wanted to give his life to God, left everything to go live in the desert with some Anchorites,[40] Stylites, and other Cenobites.[41] He was ready to lose everything in order to find God in silence and penance. Starting in the fifth century, this is how the martyrdom of some of the founders of monastic orders like St. Benedict of Nursia was recognized. People went from red martyrdom to white martyrdom. These hermits and monks bore witness to God by no longer pouring their blood for Christ, but by offering their lives to God.

In the third millennium, Pope Francis is suggesting a new way to become holy. It is in a martyrdom that is neither red nor white, but which can be called "transparent." It is transparent because the offering of their lives and complete trust in the love of God, in whom they confide, is easily seen. These saints of the new millennium allow rays of divine goodness to manifest themselves and bear witness to His love until their final gift of self. It is the martyrdom of those who offer their suffering as an offering of themselves. Pope

---

40. From the Greek anachorètes, "who withdrew from the world." This is about a kind of hermit.
41. The first monks. The Stylites meditated on top of a rock all day long, whereas the Cenobites lived in a desert community.

Francis believes this martyrdom is about the free acceptance of a "certain short-term death," that is an act of charity for others. It has to do "with a true, full, and exemplary imitation of Christ which, therefore, deserves admiration." The models are not lacking—from Anne de Guigné to Claire de Castelbajac or Chiara Corbella.[42]

This new path toward holiness recognizes that Christian virtues are sometimes lived in a heroic way in similar conditions of illness. Signs like the odor of sanctity after death often come to confirm the good death of these new saints. But it is intercession, first of all, that clearly proves that the one who has left us has not abandoned us and that like St. Thérèse, he will spend his Heaven doing good on earth.[43] Pope Francis started his *motu proprio* with this sentence from the Gospel: "Greater love has no man than this, that a man lay down his life for his friends" (John 15:13). We are called to witness to this same love by accepting persecutions, whether we offer our lives in the silence of a Carthusian monastery or in the secret of our sufferings. Carlo bore witness to this love all his life, in the offering of

---

42. Other children have not even had the words to say that they were suffering. But God, who knows the secrets of their hearts, is also acquainted with their holiness.

43. God is the first cause and the only source of our grace. But God is happy to go through secondary causes and the channels of our humanity to communicate His love. Just as it is God who is the source of life, but who goes through an intermediary—the parents, who give birth to a child—so it is God who gives grace. But He can work through the intercession of His saints.

his sickness for the souls who suffered "worse than he did" up until the end.

IN THE STEPS OF THE GREAT SAINTS

Carlo is building a bridge between Heaven and us. He was born on the earth in the '90s and was born in Heaven in the 2000s. He is building a bridge between two decades, two centuries, and two millennia. On November 24, 2016, Cardinal Angelo Scola, the archbishop of Milan, was full of praise for Carlo during the closing of the diocesan phase of his canonization cause. In his opinion, Carlo was not called to become "a movie star, but a star in Heaven" to guide and orient today's youth. He invites us to conversion through his simplicity. But if we are not prepared for transformation, we reduce his testimony to a bedtime story for children. On the contrary, Carlo's life is meant to wake us up! Today's youth must, along with Carlo, understand that holiness is still possible today. What impressed the Cardinal from Milan the most was the clarity of Carlo's life and the radiance on his face. He thought it was evident that "soon, Carlo would be raised to the altars." Carlo found perfection in the intensity of his years and not in their length. With Carlo's life, Providence places before us the example of a life that demonstrates a possible path toward holiness in the modern world. He is the "new treasure of holiness in the Ambrosian church," as

Cardinal Scola has said. Since its beginning, the Church in Milan has given the world testimonies of holiness. It was in Milan that a simple man, Ambrose, was called, by the cheering of the crowd, to become a priest and bishop of one of the first centers of Christianity. It was in Milan that Augustine, who came from Hippo in North Africa, met St. Ambrose and became a Christian. It was in Milan that Charles Borromeo, after having experienced a true conversion of heart, left all the contrivances of high-society life to become a bishop committed to the reform of his diocese after the Council of Trent. It was in Milan that another bishop, Alfredo Ildefonso Schuster, was courageous enough to invite others to fight Fascism and Communism during the Second World War. But nobody could have imagined that a holy character, who was much humbler and simpler, but also so funny and touching, would come out of Milan. Carlo was a funny saint, who loved dogs, played PlayStation, developed websites, and enjoyed going to Mass. He has not finished surprising us.

A BODY AND MORE

Among his last wishes, Carlo had asked to end his life in Assisi and be buried there. A year after his death, in 2007, his body was therefore transported to the Assisi cemetery. More than ten years later, on April 6, 2018, his body was transferred in a wooden box and brought to the Sanctuary of Spoliation (*Santuario della Spogliazione*) in Assisi in order to be more accessible to the veneration of the faithful. This church, which is in the upper part of the town, was built on the spot where St. Francis left everything to follow Christ in a life of poverty. Before the city's political and civic authorities, the young Francis, whose father opposed his vocation so that his son would take up his business in trade, stripped himself of everything in the most literal sense. He threw his clothes on the ground, as a sign of the life of poverty that he wished to pursue. We take nothing with us in death. Carlo did not take the riches of his family into his tomb. What remains today is the charity he showed the whole world. While his holiness could only be attributed to his apostolic zeal and creativity, along with the success of his Eucharistic Miracles exhibition, his burial place reminds us that holiness is not an external state, but an inner one. It is visible, not in the greatness of his works, but in his body that he wanted, at every moment, to make the Temple of the Holy Spirit.

WHEN FAITH UNFOLDS

The transfer of his relics showed, once again, the enthusiasm that surrounded young Carlo. The entire city was touched. The procession started on Friday night and resumed Saturday morning, traveling the 1.5 miles that separated the cemetery from the sanctuary. The people took a break at night in St. Rufino Cathedral. The diocesan choir sang "Not Me, but God" ("Non Io, Ma Dio"). It is a song dedicated to Carlo, composed by the artist Marco Mammoli. He is also the composer of "Emmanuel," the official hymn of World Youth Day 2000. "Non Io, ma Dio"—"Not me, but God." This is another one of Carlo's phrases that describes his life so well. The procession was not a horde of fans who came to cheer for their idol, but a crowd of Christians, many of whom, thanks to Carlo's example and intercession, rediscovered the path of faith.

In an interview with the press, an elderly lady exclaimed, "It is unbelievable that a fifteen-year-old boy would manage to attract so many people." Mrs. Teresa had not yet heard of Carlo, and these processions surprised her. Yet, she did not need see anything else to fall in love with the little Assisi saint. She said: "I am very moved to see all these young people praying around his coffin." Like her, these young people wanted to believe that Carlo was interceding for them in Heaven and that his dead body, because it had been the temple of the Holy Spirit, would also rise in glory one day.

Some people even saw a sign when, on June 23, 2018, the adolescent's body was exhumed and found to be completely integral. This rather rare phenomenon, which, if is not reserved to the saints, is, nevertheless, an astonishing sign. It is a small miracle that can sustain the faith of those who believe and test those who do not believe.

God keeps performing miracles. Yet, faith is not belief in the miracles, but in the One who is their source. Faith is the first theological virtue. It is the virtue through which we believe in God and everything that He has revealed to us, and that the Holy Catholic Church suggests that we believe because He is the truth itself.[44] We receive faith in Baptism. We repeat it each time we repeat the Creed. Faith is not believing only in Jesus' miracles, but believing in Jesus and His works. Faith is not reduced to waiting for miracles, but living the Gospel well, in accordance with virtue. A living faith transforms the life of the one who believes. God can act in him through his virtues. This is how even before a miracle was authenticated, the Holy Father recognized Carlo's heroic virtues on July 5, 2018. That day, Venerable Carlo became a hero in the faith. He is a hero who looks like us. We must hope and pray to resemble him more.

---

44. Of all the virtues, Jesus is the best model. But, since He is God, can He be a model of faith for us? As faith is a trusting surrender into the Father's hands, it finds its best model in Jesus on the Cross. Faith as a necessary virtue of imperfect knowledge discovers its model in Mary at the foot of the Cross. She did not understand everything, but received, in faith, all that God had prepared for her.

THE WORD OF GOD

Show me your faith apart from your works,
and I by my works will show you my faith.
(James 2:18)

LIFE QUESTIONS

➤ The Christian receives the Faith on the day of his Baptism. Do I know the date of my Baptism? Do I regularly give thanks to God for the gift of faith He has given to me?

➤ How do I respond when I experience doubts regarding my faith? Do the lives of the saints help give me the courage to believe?

➤ When I confront suffering, do I believe that Jesus suffers with me on the Cross? Do I think that Jesus defeated this suffering through His Resurrection?

➤ Does my faith move me to conform my life to Christ's life by loving God and neighbor, and by showing signs of our Heavenly Father's tenderness to those who suffer?

➤ Do I know the Creed, the Church's profession of faith, by heart?

PRAYER

Official Prayer for the
Canonization of Blessed Carlo Acutis

O Father, who has given us the ardent testimony of the young Venerable Carlo Acutis, who made the Eucharist the core of his life and the strength of his daily commitments so that everybody may love You above all else, let him soon be counted among the Blessed and the Saints in Your Church. Confirm my faith, nurture my hope, strengthen my charity, in the image of young Carlo, who, growing in these virtues, now lives with You. Grant me the grace that I need … I trust in You, Father, and Your Beloved Son Jesus, in the Virgin Mary, our Dearest Mother, and in the intervention of Your Venerable Carlo Acutis.

Epilogue
Interview with Antonia Salzano Acutis

Antonia, yesterday Carlo was a stranger. Today, the pope is talking about him. You were the first one to know him. You knew him, with all of a mother's love. You saw him grow up. Was Carlo an "angel" for you? Or did you only become aware of his life's extraordinary character after his death?

This dear friend, Carlo, by his nature, was not an "angel," but a simple human being. But if by "angel" you are referring to his inner qualities, then my answer to your question is yes. Throughout the Scriptures, Jesus reveals the goal to us for which all men were created. In a certain sense, we look like angels. For our vocation is to glorify God with our lives. It is specifically to love God with our whole heart and, consequently, to love our neighbor as ourselves. However, as St. Augustine said, it is not possible "that those who want to love their neighbor really love him if they have not first loved God." Carlo had this magnificent comparison. He said that on a sunny day, a clear and serene lake with pure and crystalline water reflects what surrounds it. So should it be with our soul. If it is as clear and serene as this lake, God will see the reflection of His own image while looking at it. We would often walk around the great lakes of the Milan region with Carlo. This image brings back so many memories for me. Somewhere, Carlo wrote: "To be united to Jesus forever is my program for life." I know that it is very difficult to carry out this program. It is easy to think that Carlo was not confronted with difficult objectives that the rest of us encounter when we try to implement such a big project. Nevertheless, Carlo's great virtue was to believe strongly that Jesus, through the sacraments that He instituted, effectively supports us on this voyage. He does it, in particular, through the sacraments of the Eucharist and Confession. Carlo was constantly living them.

So, what do we do to become more like Carlo, without dreaming about an angelic life?

Carlo was obviously able to see this lifestyle program through by relying on Jesus Christ. He often repeated, "The wise one is the one who always puts God first." How can we become wise like Carlo? It is, above all, by being detached from ourselves and our disordered relationships with the world, rather than aligned with the world itself. Then, we can say, with St. Paul: "Who shall separate us from the love of Christ?... Neither death, nor life ... nor anything else in all creation, will be able to separate us from the love of God in Christ Jesus our Lord" (Rom. 8:35–39). Carlo tried to follow St. Paul's exhortations to detach himself from everything and attach himself only to Christ: "It is no longer I who live (detachment), but Christ who lives in me (attachment)" (Gal. 2:20). My son wanted to attach himself exclusively to God. Carlo said that "putting God in first place meant separating yourself from everything in order to find everything in God." If you love God with all your heart, how can you be seduced by the appearance of an ordinary creature? On the contrary, every connection with people or things that we put above our connection with God will be transformed and perverted, and quickly become "idolatrous." Carlo liked to emphasize that our path on earth was covered with a thousand idols that could influence our eternal happiness. Becoming a saint in the twenty-first century is not easy. It is heroic. Heroes are just what the world and the Church need for this new millennium.

So, did Carlo have struggles. Was everything easy in his life?

Carlo experienced a struggle — yes, a struggle for holiness. Carlo said that the first thing to fight against, in order to be really *free* of every kind of bondage that takes us away from God, is a shared and imperfect love that is only half-offered. Carlo wanted to experience a holiness that would encompass his whole being. The first bondage, and the most common one, is the bondage of sin that Christ freed us from! Carlo wrote this. "What good will it do if a man has won a thousand battles if he does not manage to overcome his own corrupt passions?" Carlo thought that we experience our freedom when we are tempted. We are given the opportunity to repeat the sincerity of our love for God when we overcome our temptations without letting ourselves be distracted. He experienced trial.

Actually, Carlo seemed to have given everything to God. He spoke less of himself than of God, the Church, and the saints on every page of his life. At the same time, by completely giving of himself, he never lost himself, and was very joyful. Was it his love of God that made him so happy?

He liked to repeat that we find real happiness only in God, and that we will never be disappointed by Him: "Sadness is looking at yourself. Happiness is looking at God." We become sad each time we turn away from Him. We can already experience happiness on this earth, even if it is always imperfect, if we manage to put God in first place in our lives. He is, by definition, love. The three Divine Persons in the Holy Trinity—the Father, Son, and Holy Spirit—are united in infinite love. Man was created in the image and likeness of God. Consequently, he is naturally led to love. Only in this way can he be fulfilled and happy.

Carlo is also a model of purity for young people in the third millennium. Where does this purity come from?

Everything that distracted him from God's love was incidental. That is to say, it was not necessary in his life. If we want to live like Carlo, our whole life will consist of stripping ourselves and reducing all that is not needed for our happiness—i.e., that which obscures God's presence in us. Carlo declared that "God is very simple, and the one who wants to find Him will have to simplify himself, or else he will never find Him."

To go back to your first question, I believe that a pure man, like a pure spirit, is, above all, one who has a pure heart. It is one that is clear, transparent, simple, loyal, and faithful. He has righteous thoughts and pure intentions and is incapable of misunderstanding or deceiving. Angels are always in God's sight. We can also stand before Him if we manage to become pure in heart: "Blessed are the pure in heart, for they shall see God" (Matt. 5:8). Pure hearts have no other thoughts than those that lead directly, and almost automatically, to thinking about God. God is at the top of their priorities. God is their standard. They turn towards God. They cannot think otherwise. God is always with them and in them. Time goes by like a moment in God's presence for them. The supernatural is their atmosphere, homeland, language, and habitat. The supernatural is their measuring unit. "Seeing God" is so natural to them that it becomes almost instinctive. They think about and see

God and breathe God in. They are more from over there, Heaven, than from here. Planet Earth is their birthplace, but also and, more importantly, their point of departure for something better—the afterlife. I think that that is what Carlo experienced.

Living with a saint is probably not a bed of roses, especially when you are his mother! Normally, the parents educate the children. But have you learned anything from your son? Are you following his footsteps?

Before Carlo's birth, I was really caught up in the culture of our time. I was a prisoner of everything that is relative and limited. I was tangled up in all kinds of narrowness, boundaries, constraints, and bondages. I was living in a sort of complete unawareness, like all those slaves described by Plato in his allegory of the cave. Men and women were chained up and incapable of moving in Plato's cave. They thought that the shadows of outer things, which were reflected on the wall opposite them, were the only reality. One day, one of the prisoners finally managed to free himself from these chains and discovered the truth. That is what happened to me. Carlo showed me how to live in my century while turning toward eternity.

Yet if Carlo entered into this eternity, it must not have been easy for a mother to lose her child. How did you manage to experience this grief with such hope?

What do you want me to say? Before becoming Carlo's mother, I was not really a churchgoer or much of a believer. I went to Mass for my First Communion and returned for my Confirmation in college. I got married in the Church only after four preparatory meetings that were organized by the Italian parish in London. I was asked simply to memorize some prayers. I did not really have a personal relationship with God.

After Carlo's First Communion, the parish priest asked me if I wanted to help with a catechism class. I did not feel at all ready to do this. But I tried it anyway. Then, Carlo wanted to become a catechist. He was aware that you have to educate yourself to pass on the Faith in a better way. He started to ask me a lot of questions. When he asked me if there was a difference between the Bible and the Gospel, I did not know the answer. Together, as a family, we sought to deepen our faith to find answers to his questions.

Since Carlo was born, I have truly been awakened by the Holy Spirit. Different events have brought me closer to the Faith. I've come a long way, but I have a long way to go on this path of conversion. I started to go to church with Carlo more often, and I met some incredible priests. These were very inspired men who have brought us so much. When Carlo died, I had already traveled a beautiful path of faith. Everything happened so quickly. As a mother, I was devastated, but in faith, I did not want to despair.

When we have faith, we know that death is an encounter—a passage toward the true life where we all meet again. I have had some discouraging moments. I have been lonely. I wanted so much to have other children. Already, when Carlo was alive, my husband and I did not understand why we could not have others. We prayed and met with doctors. After four years, we joyfully gave birth to twins, Michele and Francesca. These four years of waiting were not easy, but they were enlightened by the fact that, starting with his funeral Mass, Carlo gave us signs of his presence in Heaven.

In fact, after the funeral Mass, two people bore witness to some unexplainable facts. A woman who came to this funeral Mass had a cancerous tumor. A few days later, after some blood tests, her doctor told her that the tumor had disappeared. Another woman, who was forty-four years old and never had any children, also came to this Mass. Nine months later, her insistent prayer to be able to give life was answered. These two people attributed those miracles to Carlo's intercession. Since then, it has gone *crescendo*. Today, our society is trying to forget about death. But death cannot be denied. With Jesus, death has become a passage towards life. Sooner or later, we all end up ascending Golgotha — some before others. A longer life is not necessarily a more beautiful one. What counts in the end is the love that we have had for God and our neighbor.

Thank you, Antonia. So, before wrapping up, do you want to share your most beautiful memory of Carlo in France with us?

Yes, it is our visit to the Mont-Saint-Michel in Normandy. It is so beautiful. We arrived in Normandy at night. As we were approaching this magnificent bay, we saw the Mont looming. The Archangel Michael[45] was revealed at the top of the Mont. Carlo was a fan of angels. He often prayed to his guardian angel and had a special devotion to St. Michael: "St. Michael the Archangel, defend us in battle ..." We woke up in the morning. It had snowed all night long. At dawn, we could see the Mont and the whole bay covered with a white blanket. It was splendid and very evocative. It was a marvelous moment. We also visited Chartres and Paris. We went into the Loire Valley and, of course, Lourdes. I have so many beautiful memories of these places that meant a lot to Carlo and each of us. France had a special place in his heart.

I have one last question. What, according to you, might be Carlo's key message for young people today?

Every day, I get letters from people from very diverse backgrounds. Each one is touched in his own way by the testimony of life and faith that Carlo offered. Therefore,

---

45. Mont-Saint-Michel is one of the seven sanctuaries that is dedicated to St. Michael the Archangel. From Ireland to Israel, these are situated in a perfect line that was not premeditated. We find, not only the Mount-Saint-Michel, but also Saint Michael's Abbey and the Mont Gargan sanctuary in Italy on this alignment. In this line, tradition sees the sword stroke that the Archangel Michael inflicted on the devil to send him back to Hell.

it is up to each one of us to ask ourselves this final question: What can Carlo's life change in my life? Personally, Carlo taught me to aim for God and not what is relative. He showed me the way to move out of what is not absolute to become a pilgrim of the Absolute, which is synonymous with the supernatural, but also with grace. Grace is nothing other than the recognition of the supernatural. It is about rediscovering God. Grace and the divine are connected by Calvary. Jesus, in His supreme act of love and mercy for men, gave us the greatest sacrament of His love on the Cross. Carlo taught me to place my daily routine in search of God and grace. In order to do this, we have to be continually inspired by the sacraments, especially the Eucharist, which Carlo called his "highway to Heaven." Living by aiming at what is beyond our natural world helps us to see each moment of our lives in the full light of day. This conversion can change everything. Our whole life can be turned toward Eternity.

Chronology

1991

– May 3: Birth in London.

– May 18: Carlo's Baptism.

– September: Return to Milan with his family.

1995

– September: Carlo's first day in nursery school.

1997

– September: Admittance into the elementary school of the San Carlo Institute in Milan.

1998

– January: Carlo changes grade schools and now attends Marcelline Tommaseo Institute.

– June 16: Carlo makes his First Communion in the Romites de Perego Church.

2002

– September: Admittance into the middle school of the Marcelline Tommaseo Institute.

– October: Carlo teaches his first catechism class in his parish.

2003

– May 24: Carlo makes his Confirmation at Saint-Marie Secrète Church.

2004

– Launch of Carlo's website on Eucharistic miracles.

2005

– Carlo returns to the "classical" high school of the Leo XIII Institute.

2006

– February: Carlo makes his last trip to Fatima.

– October 11: Carlo is brain dead in the San Gerardo di Monza Hospital.

– October 12: At 6:45 a.m., Carlo declared legally dead after his heart stops.

2007

– Transfer of his relics to the Assisi cemetery.

2012

– October 12: Opening of the cause for beatification and canonization by the Archdiocese of Milan.

2013

– May 13: Nihil obstat from the Congregation for the Causes of Saints.

2016

– November 24: End of the diocesan canonization process in Milan.